12 ORDINARY MEN WHO LIVED EXTRAORDINARY LIVES

A Study Guide on the Minor Prophets

DIANE RAFFERTY

ISBN 978-1-0980-8741-8 (paperback)
ISBN 978-1-0980-8742-5 (digital)

Christian Faith Publishing, Inc.
832 Park Avenue
Meadville, PA 16335
www.christianfaithpublishing.com

Printed in the United States of America

Recommended Study Aids

New American Standard Bible
(unless otherwise noted, all Scripture quotes are based on the NASB)
Maps of Old Testament Israel and surrounding
nations (back of your Bible is fine)
Halley's Bible Handbook, New Revised
Edition, Zondervan Publishing

Contents

"Grace to you and peace from God our Father and the Lord Jesus Christ. Blessed be the God and Father of our Lord Jesus Christ, who has blessed us with every spiritual blessing in the heavenly places in Christ."

"I pray that the eyes of your heart may be enlightened, so that you may know what is the hope of His calling, what are the riches of the glory of His inheritance in the saints, and what is the surpassing greatness of His power toward us who believe. These are in accordance with the working of the strength of His might."

(Ephesians 1:2–3, 18–19 NASB).

Welcome to an In-Depth Study of the Minor Prophets!

My goal in writing this study guide is for you to not only learn about the minor prophets of the Old Testament but, first and foremost, to love the entire Word of God. It is important that you understand that even though the Bible was written thousands of years ago, it is *alive* and well able to speak into your life today (Hebrews 4:12)!

Robert Morris, pastor of Gateway Church in Texas, has said that the Bible will always interpret itself.[1] If you don't understand a verse, look up the unknown word in a Bible concordance to find other places where it is used in Scripture. Read and compare the scriptures to find the meaning of the word, making sure to read the context of verses before and after it too. It is also very important that before you study the Word of God, you pray and ask the Spirit of God to open your mind and help you to understand what He wants you to learn from the text. Second Peter 1:20–21 assures us that the Spirit of God wrote all of Scripture through many different men, but the message remains the same. That is why we will use the entire Bible to study each of the twelve Old Testament books called the "Minor Prophets."

Twelve different men at varied periods of world history chronicled the specific history of the nation of Israel and the messages God gave to warn and encourage His chosen people, the Jews. These were ordinary men who were asked to do extraordinary things for God. They were people like us who had marriage problems, physical problems, emotional problems, and many were even physically harmed for speaking against the culture of the day. These books are called "Minor" because they are shorter in *length* than the "Major Prophet" books of Isaiah, Jeremiah, Ezekiel, and Daniel. For example, the book of Obadiah contains only one chapter, twenty-one verses in total and the longest book of Zechariah contains fourteen chapters. In contrast, the book of Isaiah contains sixty-six chapters. The written length of a book does not in any way correlate to the span of time (history) covered within the book. For example, the book of Micah is seven chapters long but was written over a span of sixty-plus years—an entire lifetime. Some of the books describe a single event/topic and others contain multiple topics/events in every chapter.

There is no consensus on the dates when some of these books were written, but many cite specific reigns of kings and/or events (earthquakes, famines, wars, etc.), making it easier to place the time period. The order of "Minor Prophets" as they are placed in the Bible is *not* chronological. Nine of the books were written before Israel and Judah, each went into captivity (one hundred years apart), and three books were written after the nation was again united and moved back to Jerusalem. We will study each book in the "best guess" of historical order so that we may understand the flow of world history as it intersects with the history of the nation of Israel. *Reminder: in the Old Testament, the dates get smaller into the future.*

Many of the twelve books carry the same theme of warning for the Jews to change their behavior and return to God as well as the judgment that was coming. The "Day of the Lord" is mentioned in seven of the books. Five of the books have a more personal or specific message to other nations.

The nation of Israel was split into two kingdoms after Solomon's death (1 Kings 12). Israel was in Samaria (taken captive by Assyria), and Judah (taken captive by Babylon/Chaldea) remained in Jerusalem.

It is important that prior to beginning the study, we look at the covenant God made with the nation of Israel (made up of the descendants of Jacob's twelve sons) to fully understand how badly the nation sinned and how they brought judgment upon themselves and the generations that followed.

Read Deuteronomy 28 and list all the blessings as well as all the curses that the nation agreed to in the covenant with God.

Blessings

Curses

Each Minor Prophet book contains some of these same words of blessing and cursing, and by the end of this study, you will see that *all* of these curses came to pass because the nation of Israel did *not* keep their part of the covenant.

The Book of Joel

It is very important to begin each study session with a prayer to invite the Holy Spirit of God to open your mind and heart to hear what He wants to say today.

Holy Spirit,

Thank You for inspiring the men who wrote down the words of God in these books. I agree that the Bible contains everything I need to know to live my life with peace and joy, both with God and other people. My mind and heart are open for your direction, and I will be still and quiet as I watch to see what You want to tell me today. May Your truth be a seed that is planted deep in my soul that I may change and grow more to be like Jesus. I will delight in Your Word and meditate on it day and night as You bring it to my mind. I ask this in the name of Jesus, for His glory and my good. Amen.

Author information: son of Pethuel
Meaning of his name: Yahweh (I AM) is God

Joel is considered one of the earliest prophets to Judah. The exact dates are unknown but guesstimated to be 830–750 BC during the reigns of Joash or his son Uzziah, kings of Judah.

The book of Joel is written in allegorical language. He uses word pictures to describe what he has seen and heard from the Lord. It was the Hebrew tradition to teach the next generation with stories (Psalm 78:1–8). In Joel 1:1–3, he gives a reminder for each generation to tell the next what great things God has done. The "lay people" of Joel's day did not have written scriptures, so they had to rely on the teaching of the priests in the temple.

> Allegory: A literary, dramatic, or pictorial representation;
> the apparent or superficial sense of which both
> parallels and illustrates a deeper sense.[2]

Plagues of locusts had already been experienced in Israel, so when Joel used that example to describe the invading army from the north, they could imagine the dire effect that the army would have on their city.

Locusts are an insect species of short-horned grasshoppers that have swarming phases. They are usually solitary, but under certain circumstances they become more abundant and change their behavior and habits. When grouped together, they are called a swarm of locust and they create disaster wherever they go as they devour all green plants (grass, trees, crops, etc.) in their path. Such plagues of locust have occurred throughout history all over the world and still happen today. (See Exodus 10:12–19.)[3]

Write the description of the enemy from the north given in Joel 1:1–6, 2:1–4.

What will they do (Joel 1:7–12, 16–20, 2:5–9)?

> Ancient war tactics: Strip all the good stuff: food supplies—livestock, crops, etc.; transportation: horses, carts, wagons etc.; wealth: gold, silver, jewels, etc. Burn everything behind you—results in drought and famine which leaves more death and destruction behind.

What does God tell His people to do (Joel 1:8, 11, 13, 14, 2:12–17)?

What does God promise to do (Joel 2:18–27, 3:16–21)?

> God is *always* willing and ready to restore His people *but* repentance *must* come first!

God would bring the northern army (Babylon/Chaldea) to bring judgment/correction to His people. Just as the locust were both real, swarms, as well as an allegorical description of a real army, so too is the "Day of the Lord." It was used to describe the actual day of a future invasion as well as the future events found in the book of Revelation to describe when Jesus will come back to earth in a final war with the nations.

Describe the Day of the Lord: (Joel 2:2–11, 30–32; Isaiah 13:9–13; Revelation 6:12–17)

THE BOOK OF JOEL

Description of the locust/enemy in Revelation 9:1–11

Who will be judged (Joel 3:2, 4, 9, 12, 14, 19)?

Why are they judged (Joel 3:2–6, 19, 21)?

How and where will they be judged (Joel 3:2, 7–14, Revelation 16:13–21, 19:17–21)?

What is said about the wine press (Joel 3:13, Revelation 14:14–20, 19:11–16)?

> *Important note:* This army of demon locust is *not* allowed
> to kill anyone, only cause torment. Satan and his fallen
> angels (demons) have *no* authority to kill you either, but
> they are quite good at talking people into killing themselves
> (suicide) and others (murder). Satan *only* has the power
> that *you give* to him. Jesus already took it back!

Life Application

What does the message of this prophet have to do with my life today?

Do you need to fast, weep, mourn, or repent of some sin that is taking over your life? Do it now. Jesus has already paid for it on the cross. You only need to believe, receive, and walk out of it into victory now.

Can you think of a time of loss in your life when you felt that God had "stripped it bare"? God's promise of restoration is for you (Joel 2:23–26). Write His promise in your own words to fit your situation.

In Acts 2:14–21, Peter quotes from Joel 2:28–32 and says that this scripture has been fulfilled. What happens when the Spirit comes into your life at salvation (Isaiah 44:3; Joel 2:28–29; Acts 2:1–18, 33, 39, 15:8–9, 19:6)?

What does God say about prophecy in the life of the believer today (Amos 3:7–8; 1 Corinthians 12:3–11, 14:3, 36–40; Ephesians 4:11–12; 2 Thessalonians 5:19–21; 2 Peter 1:19–21)?

In the book *Speak Life*, Pastor Brady Boyd describes modern prophets as people who hear God's message for another person and pass the information on to him or her. In order to hear God's input for others, Pastor Brady encourages us, *while we are in conversation with people, to ask the Holy Spirit what He wants to say to this person.*[4]

How exciting and radically changed would our lives be if all of God's people would open up the line of Spirit-led communication while we go about our daily lives, interacting with people who need to hear from God?

Caution

It is wise to first ask a person if you can share the information that you are receiving from the Spirit for them. If possible always use scripture to speak as we are told in 2 Timothy 3:16, that it is the Word of God that has the power to change lives and in Isaiah 55:11, God says that His words will accomplish and succeed in the purpose for which they have been sent.

The Spirit of God does not give gifts based upon our sex or natural talents and abilities. He gives gifts without partiality to those who are willing to hear His voice and act on what they hear. You must believe that God still speaks and that He has something He wants to say to encourage and build up His children. All the gifts of the Spirit are to be used to build His kingdom and to bring glory and honor to Jesus and God the Father.

Bonus study: Women who prophesied in the Bible: Exodus 15:20–21, Judges 4:4–5, 2 Kings 22:14–20, 2 Chronicles 34:22–28, Nehemiah 6:14, Luke 2:36–38, Acts 21:9.

Encouragement

"For whom God has sent speaks the words of God; for He gives the Spirit without measure." (John 3:34 NASB)

"Now we have received, not the spirit of the world, but the Spirit who is from God, that we might know the things freely given to us by God, which things we also speak not in words taught by human wisdom, but in those taught by the Spirit, combining spiritual thoughts with spiritual words." (1 Corinthians 2:12–13 NASB)

"For I long to see you in order that I may impart some spiritual gift to you, that you may be established; that is, that I may be encouraged together with you while among you, each of us by the other's faith, both yours and mine." (Romans 1:11–12 NASB)

Closing Summary

The book of Joel is a warning of the day of coming judgment and a call for national and individual repentance. Are you ready?

It is also a reminder of God's promise that He can and will restore to His people everything that the enemy (Satan) has stolen and destroyed in their lives. Ask God for restoration in those areas of your life and believe the promise is for you today!

The promised "latter rain" of the Spirit of God was given to the early church and the Spirit continues to "rain" on *believers* today.

"Although the Lord has given you bread of privation and water of oppression, He, your Teacher will no longer hide Himself, but your eyes will behold your Teacher. And your ears will hear a word behind you, "This is the way, walk in it," whenever you turn to the right or the left." (Isaiah 30:20–21 NASB)

"What I tell you in the darkness, speak in the light; and what you hear whispered in your ear, proclaim upon the housetops." (Matthew 10:27 NASB)

"He who has ears to hear, let him hear." (Matthew 11:15 NASB)

Are you willing to hear Him today?
Are you willing to speak to others on His behalf?

Challenge for the Week

Practice Spirit-led communication in all of your conversations/interactions with others. Listen for what the Spirit has to say to you and speak it out loud to encourage someone today!

Recommended Reading on Prophecy and How to Hear God's Voice

Speak Life by Brady Boyd, David C Cook publishing
Walking with God: How to Hear His Voice by John Eldridge, Thomas Nelson publishing
Seeing the Voice of God by Laura Harris Smith, Chosen publishing

The Book of Amos

It is very important to begin each study session with a prayer to invite the Holy Spirit of God to open your mind and heart to hear what He wants to say today.

Holy Spirit,

Thank You for inspiring the men who wrote down the words of God in these books. I agree that the Bible contains everything I need to know to live my life with peace and joy, both with God and other people. My mind and heart are open for Your direction, and I will be still and quiet as I watch to see what You want to tell me today. May Your truth be a seed that is planted deep in my soul that I may change and grow more to be like Jesus. I will delight in Your Word and meditate on it day and night as You bring it to my mind. I ask this in the name of Jesus, for His glory and my good. Amen.

Meaning of his name: To lift a burden, carry. This shortens to "burden bearer" (an apt name for him).

Read Amos 1:1, 7:14–15.

Unlike some other Minor Prophet writers, Amos was a sheepherder and farmer of fig trees (sycamore) from the city of Tekoa. He was a "layman" and not a priest or prophet by trade. Amos lived at the same time as Jonah, Elisha, and perhaps even Joel.[5]

Jeroboam II was king of Israel at the time of writing. It had been some two hundred years since the nation of Israel had split into two kingdoms: Israel to the north with its capital in Samaria and Judah to the south with its capital in Jerusalem. During this time God had sent Elijah, Elisha, and Jonah, but Israel paid no attention and continued on their downward path. God sent Amos in a final effort to get them to turn back. He actually lived in the southern kingdom of

21

Judah, but God gave him messages to the northern kingdom of Israel as well as the surrounding nations.[6]

> Tekoa (a city in the wilderness [2 Chronicles 20:20])
> is thought to be the same region where John the
> Baptist grew up eight hundred years later.[7]

Amos was obviously a gifted communicator because in this book, he uses several different writing styles to convey God's messages. Just as Joel wrote using visual pictures to help the listener understand the Lord's message, so too Amos uses everyday examples from his own life, i.e., shepherds, pastures, farming tools, trees, and animals etc.

> In all areas of ministry, God works within the parameters of
> a person's occupation, life experiences, and personality type.
> God has designed each of us individually in our mother's
> womb, and we all have a special role to play in the kingdom!

Amos also wrote in poetic rhythm "for three transgressions and for four…" In the first two chapters, he gives specific warnings of judgment (woes) to eight different nations. An easy way to remember the list of nations is the acronym GATED JIM. Look for the location of each nation on maps located in the back of your Bible.

G is for GAZA = Philistines (Ashdod, Ashkelon, Ekron) (Amos 1:6–8, 2; Chronicles 21:16–17; Zephaniah 2:4–5; Jeremiah 47:4–5a; Ezekiel 25:15–17).

What is the reason for God's punishment? And how were they punished?

A is for AMMON = *Rabbah* (Amos 1:13–15; Isaiah 13:15–18; Jeremiah 49:1–6)

What is the reason for God's punishment? And how were they punished?

T is for Tyre = *Seacoast nation* (Amos 1:9; Ezekiel 26:2, 7, 14, 19; Isaiah 23:13–15)

What is the reason for God's punishment? And how were they punished?

E is for Edom=Esau's descendants—cousins of the nation of Israel (Arabian Desert) (Amos 1:11; Numbers 20:18; 2 Chronicles 20:22–23, 28:17; Isaiah 34:6b–15; Jeremiah 49:7–22). (Note: the entire book of Obadiah is about Edom [Esau] and its treatment of Israel.)

What is the reason for God's punishment? And how were they punished?

> Teman is the grandson of Esau. Firstborn son of the firstborn son who became a chief of the Edom clan (Genesis 36:11, 15). Mount Teman is named after him.

D is for Damascus = *Syria* (Amos 1:3; Isaiah 7:8; 1 Kings 22:3–35; 2 Kings 8:12–13, 16:7–9).

What is the reason for God's punishment? And how were they punished?

J is for Judah = *Jerusalem* (Amos 2:4; 2 Kings 17:19, 25:8–11; 2 Chronicles 33:11, 36:17–20).

What is the reason for God's punishment? And how were they punished?

I is for Israel = *Samaria* (Amos 2:6; 1 Kings 12:28–33; 2 Kings 17:6–23).

What is the reason for God's punishment? And how were they punished?

M is for Moab = *Kir in the Arabian desert* (Amos 2:1–3; Isaiah 15:1–9, 16:14; Zephaniah 2:9).

What is the reason for God's punishment? And how were they punished?

All of these prophesies were fulfilled within fifty years.[8]

Throughout chapters 3–7, Amos uses legal language and argues his "case" as in a court of law with God sitting as the judge.

Chapter 3. List his logical questions in verses 3–8

Note God's answer in verses 11–15

"they do not know how to do what is right." (Amos 3:10a NASB)

Chapter 4. Meet Your God.

What did God do to get their attention (verses 6–11)?

The region of Bashan (4:1) was famous for its cattle
industry[9] (see Psalm 22:12; Ezekiel 39:18).

Who is this God (Amos 4:13 and 5:8–9)?

Chapter 5. Seek the Lord that you may live…or else what (verses 4–7,
14)?

God always leaves a remnant of 10 percent—a tithe
of the nation (Amos 5:3; Revelation 7:4, 14:4)

Amos 5:18 says that the people were longing for the "Day of the
Lord," but they had no real concept of the horror of that day. Things
will get worse, not better! List the descriptions given in verses 18–20:

List the sins of the people and the reasons they would go into exile
(verses 21–26).

These festivals and sacrifices were the ones that Jeroboam I created in place of those God had ordained with the addition of worship of the golden calves and stars (Saturn, etc.) (1 Kings 12:25–33).

Chapter 6. Warnings to the Rich and Proud. Describe the people and their lifestyle below.

Definitions: Lo-debar = a thing of nothing[10]
Wormwood = bitter plant which grows in wastelands[11]

What member of a royal family lived in Lo-debar? Read 2 Samuel 9.

Chapter 7. Amos argues with God.

What was God's judgment, Amos's argument, and the result in verses 1–3?

What was God's judgment, Amos's argument, and the result in verses 4–6?

God's character NEVER changes, but He is willing to show mercy and relent (soften His anger) toward those that turn to Him.

Bonus study: Does God change? Compare Malachi 3:6, 1 Samuel 15:29, Numbers 23:19, Genesis 18:17–33, Exodus 32:11–14, Jeremiah 26:13,19, and Jonah 3:9, 4:2, 11.

What did God use to take the measure of Israel (verses 7–9)?

Do you know what a plumb line is? A plumb line is used to take a vertical (up and down) measurement to ensure whatever you are building is straight (not leaning or crooked). God holds the plumb line of His law against the actions of the people of Israel and they do not line up straight at all. Therefore, the "building" of Israel must be taken down. See Isaiah 28:16–17.

Bethel was the location for one of the golden calves that Jeroboam I set up for Israel to worship (the other one was in Dan, 1 Kings 12:26–29). Amaziah was called "the priest of Bethel" but he was not God's priest (from the tribe of Levi). Jeroboam I had chosen Amaziah to serve as a priest to his royal household. Therefore when Amos was in Bethel prophesying against Jeroboam (verse 11), Amaziah complained to the king and tried to chase Amos back to Judah (verse 12).

What was Amos's response to this verbal attack (verses 14–17)?

No one can stop you if/when God has given you something to do/ say. You don't need a title or label to represent God (pastor, priest, etc.). *God uses people who are humble and willing to obey Him!*

Chapter 8. Day of Judgment/famine of the WORD.

Who are represented as bad fruit and what did they do (verses 1–6)?

Scholars believe that Amos wrote this book of prophesy at least two years later when he was visiting in Bethel. That is why in Amos 8:8 and 9:5, he foretells of an earthquake, and in Amos 1:1, he states that he saw these prophetic visions two years before the earthquake happened.[12]

What will the "Day of the Lord" be like (verses 8–10)?

Compare the day of Jesus's death on the cross (God's only Son) noted in Matthew 27:45–56 to Amos 8:8–10. How are they the same?

In verses 11–14, it talks about a famine, not for bread or a thirst for water, but a famine and drought for hearing the words of the Lord. This famine/drought was broken by Jesus Himself. See what John 1:1, 4:10, and 6:35 say about this.

No words written after the book of Malachi until Jesus's birth in the Gospels were included in the Bible. Four hundred years![13]

Chapter 9. Nowhere to hide: God's judgment is unavoidable.

THE BOOK OF AMOS

How will the people try to escape judgment and who will die (verses 1–10; Revelation 6:12–17)?

Verses 11–12 speak of the future church that is made up of both Jews and Gentiles and called by Jesus's name—Christians (Acts 11:19–26). The fallen booth of David is the earthly kingdom that has gone astray, but when Jesus came, He talked of a new heavenly kingdom. Amos 9:13–15 and Revelation 21 through 22:5 describe the new kingdom and new earth where Jesus will reign forever.

Life Application and Closing Summary

What does the message of this prophet have to do with my life today? The book of Amos is all about warnings and what will happen to those who do not repent and turn to God for Salvation. Amos 5:10 NASB says that *"They hate him who reproves in the gate, And abhor those who speak with integrity."* and 5:13 NASB says, *"at such a time the prudent person keeps silent, for it is an evil time."*

Do you think this time in history is an evil time? Why or why not?

Do you speak out when you see sin or do you think it is a time to be quiet? Why or why not?

We often judge Israel and Judah harshly because they fell so far away from God's laws by adding their own ideas/wishes to it. (Remember the agreement in Deuteronomy 28.) In what ways have you added to God's law or ignored it entirely in order to fit in with the world around you in the following areas?

Abortion

Pre-marital sex

Adultery

Divorce

Same-sex marriage

Horoscope/palm reading

Pornography

TV/movies with nudity/violence/foul talk

Gossip/slander

Disrespect of elders/parents

Working every day and taking no Sabbath day to honor/spend time alone with God

Facebook time instead of/or more time with than the "Good Book"—Bible

Challenge for the Week

The day of the Lord's judgment *is* coming. Are you ready to face Him or do you need to repent and turn back to following His *Word*, both written (Bible) and living (Jesus and Holy Spirit)?

Prayer of Repentance (say aloud)

Dear God,

Thank You for showing me my sin of_____.
I confess that I haven't measured up to Your Word, and today I am committing myself to turn away from this sin through the power of Your Spirit who lives in me. I thank You, Jesus, that You have washed me with Your blood and removed all my guilt and shame that You took on Yourself at the cross. I bind any demon influences that may

have entered my heart and mind and I cast them out in the authority of the name of Jesus. I commit myself to fill my heart and mind with Your Word. Spirit, I ask that You help me to say no to myself and yes to You as You guide and direct my steps in the way that I should walk today. Amen.

The Book of Jonah

It is very important to begin each study session with a prayer to invite the Holy Spirit of God to open your mind and heart to hear what He wants to say today.

Holy Spirit

Thank You for inspiring the men who wrote down the words of God in these books. I agree that the Bible contains everything I need to know to live my life with peace and joy, both with God and other people. My mind and heart are open for Your direction and I will be still and quiet as I watch to see what You want to tell me today. May Your truth be a seed that is planted deep in my soul, that I may change and grow more to be like Jesus. I will delight in Your Word and meditate on it day and night as You bring it to my mind. I ask this in the name of Jesus, for His glory and my good. Amen.

Author information: Jonah was a prophet from Gath-hepher in the northern kingdom of Israel, son of Amittai. His prophecy is also mentioned in 2 Kings 14:23–25 as being fulfilled by King Jeroboam II.

Meaning of his name: Dove.

Jonah was a contemporary of the prophet Elisha and was just before the time of Hosea and Micah. At the time of this prophecy, the kingdom of Assyria was violently taking over all the surrounding nations. They now ruled from what would become the Babylonian Empire and their capital city was Nineveh. Just the name Assyria struck terror into people's hearts, so when God told Jonah to go to Nineveh and preach a warning of coming judgment, He was naturally scared and unwilling.[14]

The story of "Jonah and the Whale" is well-known, even to those who haven't read the Bible and many believe that it is just that—a story. What the book of Jonah really is is a very raw and personal diary of one man's emotional struggles to obey the call of God on his life, no matter what it cost him personally, and just like most of us, Jonah made it more difficult for himself than God ever intended.

Since the story itself is so well-known, we will be looking at five lessons for our lives today based on this very personal journal that shows the good, the bad, and sometimes the ugliness of Jonah's inner personal life with God.

Jonah is human. When he doesn't want to do something God tells him to do, he thinks of all the reasons not to and then makes his own plan of action. He left home, traveled south to Joppa, where he bought a ticket for a boat traveling to Tarshish (located in modern-day country of Spain). Rationally, he probably told himself that it was "fate" when he found he could afford a ticket on a ship leaving that day and going in the opposite direction of Nineveh.

> Perfect circumstances do *not* equal God's will!
> "There is a way which SEEMS right to a man, but its end is the way of death" (Proverbs 14:12 NASB) (Emphasis mine).

Lesson 1: You cannot go anywhere that God is not already there (Jonah 1:1–3). Compare to Psalm 139:7–10, Jeremiah 23:24, Hebrews 4:13, Romans 8:38–39. How does this apply to your life with God?

Question to ponder: "Did God really say..." (Genesis 3:1–6)?

Have you ever had God speak to you so clearly that you knew what you were supposed to do/not do but the more time you let go by, the more your reasoning talked you out of it? What was the end result?

Read Joshua 1:7 and 9 to see what you should have thought instead.

> The moment that God tells you to do something means that there is an anointing power to do it. God knows the right timing for everything, and we must trust and obey Him in that moment to ensure success. When we put things off and wait for our own timing, it may no longer have the anointing power because of our disobedience.

Lesson 2: Our sin has an effect on other people's lives, but God can make good things happen out of our bad actions.

Compare Jonah 1:4–16, Genesis 20:9–18, Genesis 45:5–8 and list who sinned, who else was affected by it, and what good God brought in the end.

Question to ponder: What dumb things have you done that have harmed other people? How have you seen God bring good from a bad situation?

"And we know that God causes *all* things to work together for good to those who love God, to those who are called according to *His* purpose." (Romans 8:28 NASB) (Emphasis mine).

Casting lots was like throwing the dice—believing that the number/symbols would direct their next step/action. The Christian does not need to do this because the Spirit of God lives inside of us and He will direct our next steps if we ask and take the time to listen.

Bonus study on casting lots: Psalm 22:18, Matthew 27:35, Leviticus 16:8, Numbers 26:55, 33:54, Joshua 18:8–10, 1 Samuel 14:41–42, Esther 3:7, 1 Chronicles 24:5, Nehemiah 10:34, Proverbs 16:33, 18:18, Acts 1:26.

Lesson 3: God forgives a prayer of repentance but the consequences of sin remain.

It is thought that because Jonah was in the fish's stomach for three days, the stomach acids probably bleached not only his clothing but his skin and hair.[15] He was forever changed on the outside as much as he was on the inside when he thought he was going to die. Sometimes it takes an awful/scary event in our lives to cause us to repent of our own ways and go the way God has laid out for us.

Read these scriptures and write down the person, their sin, and what consequences they had to deal with.

Jonah 2:1–10

Genesis 3:17–24

Numbers 20:8–12; Deuteronomy 32:50–52

2 Samuel 12:13–14

Question to ponder: What sin have you committed that has had a lasting result and changed your life forever?

How has it affected your life with God?

Read Psalm 51, which is David's prayer of repentance after killing Uriah and the death of his child. Write out a prayer of repentance of your sin using your own words.

Lesson 4: If you want to hear more from God, you need to do the last thing He told you to do.

Read Jonah 3:1–3. We aren't told how much time has passed from the first call of God to the second one other than Jonah's three days in the fish. Depending on where the fish spit him up on the beach, he probably still had a long walk to Nineveh. During this time he hears from the Lord a second time. "Same song, second verse, a little bit louder and a whole lot worse..." as the song goes. Jonah must have felt fear and dread rising again in his heart, but this time we are told that he arose and went to Nineveh. The message wasn't as specific as it was in Jonah 1:2. This time God says to proclaim a message that *"I am going to tell you."* God always asks us for obedience without needing to know all the details (2 Corinthians 5:7—we walk by faith, not by sight). Jonah had to arrive at Nineveh before he got the actual message to speak.

Compare these scriptures to see what Abraham and Elijah were told to do by faith without knowing all the details: Genesis 12:1, 13:1, 14; 1 Kings 17:3–16, 18:1.

Abraham

Elijah

Elijah sets a good example for our lives today. He waited until he had a clear word from God and then he did exactly what he was told to do. He stayed where God put him until he had a further word from God to move on.

Question to ponder: When was the last time you felt you had a word from God? Did you obey? Have you ever moved on before God told you to, or have you remained past the time He told you to leave?

I have personally experienced what happens if you remain when God has told you to leave. You no longer enjoy where you are and it starts to get uncomfortable, things go wrong, and soon you can't wait to get out and/or others can't wait for you to leave. Remember, God's timing is *always* the right timing!

Lesson 5: Our job is to obey; the results are up to God. Read Jonah 3:5–10.

According to historical records, the city of Nineveh was about thirty miles long and ten miles wide. It was protected by five walls and three moats/canals built by the forced labor of thousands of foreign captives. In Jonah 3:3, we are told that it was an "exceedingly great city" and would take three days to walk through it.[16]

Remember that while Jonah is walking through the city, he is not only yelling (cried out) a scary message of destruction and death but he looked scary too! I'm sure that the sight of him alone with his skin bleached white with burned or scarred patches, his black hair being bleached blond or perhaps even orange, maybe even falling out in places, he was scary to see as well as to hear. God truly can take our sin and bring good out of it. Everyone must have stopped to stare when they saw Jonah, and it gave him time to speak God's message to a very quiet audience who weren't too sure what/who they were looking at.

Everyone in the city was talking about this strange man and his message from an unknown God. People began responding to the message by fasting and wearing sackcloth. The city was in such an uproar that the king heard about it and he and his nobles also laid aside their fine clothing and put on sackcloth and sat on ashes to show their repentance. The king issued a royal decree to also fast from food and water; even their animals were to wear sackcloth! They totally believed the warning of Jonah and God relented.

Fasting is a deliberate abstinence from physical gratification—usually going without food or drink for a set amount of time to achieve a greater spiritual goal. Intentionally denying the flesh in order to gain a response from the Spirit. Renouncing the natural in order to invoke the supernatural.[17]

Sackcloth and ashes from the fireplace were worn to show sorrow— in this case sorrow for their sin. It was an external demonstration of an internal condition. Clothing was also often torn to show that they were emotionally torn up as well.

Bonus study on fasting: 2 Samuel 1:11–12; 1 Kings 21:25–29; Joel 2:12–13, Esther 4:1, 16; Daniel 9:3–8; Acts 13:2–3, 14:23; Matthew 4:2, 17:14–21.

God's character *never* changes, but He is willing to show mercy and relent (see Jeremiah 18:7–10).

In Jonah 4:11 NASB, God asks Jonah, "Should I not have compassion on Nineveh, the great city in which there are more than 120,000 persons who do not know the difference between their right and left hand, as well as many animals?" This number alludes to the babies and young children. Consider how many older children and adults that lived in the city and its surroundings. Some scholars put the number close to one million people, and isn't it interesting that God cared for the lives of the animals as well?

What do these scriptures say about God's judgment and mercy? Psalm 7:11–12, 9:7–8, Jeremiah 18:8–10, Romans 5:6–8, 9:15–16.

Lesson 6: God can even use people who are not quite emotionally stable.

Read Jonah 4:1–11 and list all of the emotions Jonah displayed.

The plant that grew up quickly is thought to be the castor oil plant that is commonly grown in Palestine for its shade. It grows rapidly and has large leaves but easily dies if/when the stem is injured.[18]

Describe the emotional roller coaster of these other people that were used by God for His purpose:

Saul: 1 Samuel 13:8–14, 14:24–30, 43–45, 15:17–30, 18:1–12, 20:30–33, 24:9–22, 26:17–21, 31:1–4

David: Psalm 42

Elijah: 1 Kings 17:1, 20–23, 18:16, 19:14; 2 Kings 1:8–15, 2 Kings 2:1–11

Peter: Matthew 14:26–31, 16:15–19, 17:4–6, 26:31–35; Mark 8:32–33; John 18:10–18, 25–27, 21:7–21; Acts 2:14, 3:4–7, 4:8–12, etc.

Question to ponder: Do you believe that God can use you even though He knows the "real" you? Think about the people in the Bible who did dumb things and/or acted badly. God forgave them and used them to bless future generations…so why not you?

Life Application and Closing Summary

What does the message of this prophet have to do with my life today?
The book of Jonah should be considered an excerpt taken out of a journal/diary, written about a specific time in his life. Jonah was very open and honest with his emotions, fears, courage, bad attitudes, etc. If you were to write a journal of your life, would you be willing to write it *all* down?

We must always remember that the Holy Spirit of God is the author of all that is in the Bible and He decides what will be written, not the men who wrote the books. What would our lives be like if the Bible didn't contain people like Saul, Elijah, Jonah, or Peter? If we were to read only about people who did everything right, we couldn't relate. God sent Jesus to earth because *every* human being is "flawed" and in need of a Savior. We are in good company with Jonah and the others.

Note: There is still a mound near Nineveh that is called "Yunas Mound" = Tomb of Jonah. Don't ever think that your life won't have a lasting effect on the people around you. God is able to do anything *with a life that is given to Him.*[19]

Challenge for the Week

Take the book of Jonah and rewrite it in your own words as a personal diary and see if you can better relate to what he went through, both physically and emotionally. Ask the Spirit if there is any area where you have been running away, causing others to sin, not having compassion for others, etc., and resolve to allow God to change you today by the power of the Holy Spirit within you.

Memorize and/or write out and read daily: Colossians 3:12–17.

For more interesting information on Jonah and the whale, go to: www.gotquestions.org/Jonah-whale.html

Modern-Day Jonah Story

I was watching *Mysteries of the Deep* with host Jeremy Wade on the Discovery Channel the other night (7/28/20) and he shared a story of a photographer who was scuba diving off the coast of South Africa in March 2019. The diver was swallowed by a "Bryde's whale." These whales have no teeth as they eat mostly krill and small fish (www.whalefacts.org/brydes-whale-facts/). The diver spent a few anxious minutes inside the whale's mouth but was then let go without being harmed. Wade theorized that since this type of whale uses echo location to help them find food, when the photographer was focusing on a large school of sardines, the whale may not have been able to discern the difference between him and the fish ball. It shows that whales have big enough mouths to fit an entire human being and that there are types who would not eat a human because they have no teeth to chew them up. Interesting!

The Book of Micah

It is very important to begin each study session with a prayer to invite the Holy Spirit of God to open your mind and heart to hear what He wants to say today.

Holy Spirit,

Thank You for inspiring the men who wrote down the words of God in these books. I agree that the Bible contains everything I need to know to live my life with peace and joy, both with God and other people. My mind and heart are open for Your direction and I will be still and quiet as I watch to see what You want to tell me today. May Your truth be a seed that is planted deep in my soul, that I may change and grow more to be like Jesus. I will delight in Your Word and meditate on it day and night as You bring it to my mind. I ask this in the name of Jesus, for His glory and my good. Amen.

Author information: Micah was from the city of Moresheth in the days of Jotham, Ahaz, and Hezekiah—kings of Judah. The most interesting thing about the book of Micah is that the seven chapters contain over sixteen different messages given over a period of sixty-plus years. We know this because of all the kings that are listed.

2 Kings 15:32–34	Jotham, son of Uzziah, twenty-five years old	sixteen years	good king
2 Kings 15:27	Pekah	twenty years	bad king
2 Kings 16:1–3	Ahaz, son of Jotham, twenty years old	sixteen years	bad king

| 2 Kings 17:1–6 | Hoshea | until taken away by Assyria | nine years | bad king |
| 2 Kings 18:1–3 | Hezekiah, son of Ahaz, twenty-five years old | | twenty-nine years | bad king |

Meaning of his name: Who is like the LORD?

As noted above, there are many stops and starts in the writing of Micah's prophecy. The topic jumps back and forth over time and themes, so in this lesson, they will be grouped by subject/theme for ease of study. His messages of judgment are for Israel (Samaria) and Judah (Jerusalem).

If your Bible has a map section at the back, check to see if you can find the towns where Micah lived and preached from the list below (Micah 1:10–15). (Some may not be shown on your map.)

Bethlaphrah	House of dust—roll in the dirt, humility, mourning
Shaphir	Pleasantness—instead go into captivity in shame
Zaanan	Going out—everyone has to leave; no one escapes
Bethezel	House of removal—no one can stand against God's wrath and the Assyrian army
Maroth	Bitterness—become weak waiting for any good to come
Lachish	Who walks or exists—one of the last two fortified cities in Judah (Jeremiah 34:7)
Moresheth-gath	Possession of the wine press—Micah's hometown
Achzib	Place of deceit—one of the cities given to tribe of Judah near a water source (Joshua 15:44)
Mareshah	Possession—one of the cities given to tribe of Judah near a water source (Joshua 15:44)
Adullam	Glory of God would be hidden—Refuge where David hid from Saul (1 Samuel 22:1)

List the sins of the rich/rulers found in the verses from Micah below:

2:1, 7:3

2:2–4

2:7

2:9

3:1, 11, 7:3

3:3

3:9

6:10–12

7:2

Bonus study on cannibalism during sieges and famine in the Bible: Micah 3:2–3; Deuteronomy 28:49–58; Leviticus 26:25–29; 2 Kings 6:24–28; Jeremiah 19:9; Lamentations 2:20, 4:1–10; Ezekiel 5:10.

List the judgments of God on the rich/rulers found in these verses from Micah:

1:6–7

1:16

3:12

5:1–11

6:14–16

7:5–6

List the sins of the *false* priests and prophets in the verses below:

3:5

5:12–14

6:7

6:16 (sins of Jeroboam, Omri and Ahab: 1 Kings 12:25–33, 13:33–34, 16:25–26, 30–33)

List the judgments of God on the *false* priests and prophets in Micah 3:6–7:

Bonus study on the evil practice of child sacrifice: Leviticus 18:21, 20:2–5; Exodus 22:29; Deuteronomy 18:10; 2 Kings 16:3, 17:6–8, 17, 21:1, 6; 2 Chronicles 28:3, 33:1, 6; Psalm 106:35–38; Isaiah 57:5; Jeremiah 7:31, 32:35, Ezekiel 16:20–21, 20:26, 31, 23:37.

Assyria = The land of Nimrod (Babylon) (Genesis 10:8–12)

Write your thoughts about the judgments of Israel and Judah listed below:

Judgment of Israel (Samaria), 722–721 BC. People were exiled to Assyria in 734 BC.
Micah 1:6–7, 5:5–6; 2 Kings 16:6–13, 16–17 (2 Kings 16:8 = Micah 1:14 "parting gifts")

Judgment of Judah (Jerusalem), 606 BC. People were exiled to Babylon (during the one hundred years between judgments, Assyria's power waned and the Babylonian/Chaldeans rose to power.)
Micah 1:9, 13, 16, 2:12–13, 3:12, 4:10, 5:1; 2 Kings 25:1–21; 2 Chronicles 36:7–8, 10, 15–20

List the future events in Micah 4:3–7:

> Note: Micah 4:1–2 is almost word for word with
> Isaiah 2:2–4. Same Spirit = Same message!

List the future events foretold about Jesus the Messiah (Micah 5:2–5).

Did you know that Jesus and the Holy Spirit were also at creation with God the Father? Read Genesis 1:1–27 and John 1:1–5, Colossians 1:15–17.

"His goings forth are from long ago…" in Micah 5:2c NASB refers to the many times in the Old Testament where Jesus appeared and talked to people. Any time you see "The Angel of the LORD" or one "like the Son of God," it refers to Jesus visiting the earth before He came as a baby. This is called a "theophany."

Who did Jesus appear to in the following texts?

Genesis 14:18–20 (Some scholars believe this was Jesus) (Hebrews 7:1–6)

Genesis 18

Judges 6:11–22

Daniel 3:24–28

Comments Micah Makes about Himself

Micah 1:8. Note how God required Micah to be visually different to draw attention to himself and his message (just like Jonah).

How has God caused you to be different from those around you so that they would pay more attention to the role God has in your life and what you say about God?

Micah 3:8. Micah needed courage to walk around almost naked and yelling about sin and judgment in the face of all the lies the false priests were telling to the people. Write out what he said below.

David also gave himself pep talks to build himself up in the Lord. Read Psalm 42:11 and use it for yourself!

Even though Micah's days were lonely and he could feel the darkness of sin, he still got his courage and confidence in God. He gave himself a pep talk whenever he got too low over the many years he prophesied and waited for it to be fulfilled.

Micah 7:7. What are the three "I will" statements that Micah makes in this verse?

1.
2.
3.

Comments Micah Makes about God

Micah 2:7b NASB: "Is the Spirit of the Lord impatient? "Do not MY WORDS do good to the one walking uprightly?" (Emphasis mine)

Micah 4:2b NASB: "That He may teach us about His ways and that we may walk in His paths." (Read Psalm 25:4–5)

Micah 4:12a NASB: "But they do not know the thoughts of the LORD and they do not understand His purpose." (Read Isaiah 55:8–9; Romans 11:33)

Micah 6:8 NASB: "He has told you, O man, what is good; And what does the LORD require of you but to do justice, to love kindness, and to walk humbly with your God?" (Read Psalm 89:14)

Micah 7:15 NASB: "As in the days when you came out from the land of Egypt, I will show you miracles." (Read Matthew 11:21–24 [Jesus] Acts 5:12 [Apostles] Acts 19:11–12 [Paul]).

God is the *same* yesterday, today, and forever!

Micah 7:18–19: Who is a God like you?
Who:

- Pardons iniquity
- Passes over rebellious acts
- Does not stay angry forever
- Delights in unchanging love
- Will have compassion on us
- Will tread our iniquities under His feet
- Will cast *all* of our sins into the depths of the sea

Read these verses and write down a prayer of thankfulness to God in your own words: Jeremiah 31:34, 32:37–41; Psalm 103:10–13.

Bonus study when God touches the earth = earthquakes: Exodus 19:18, Judges 5:4–5, 1 Kings 19:11, Psalm 68:8, Ezekiel 38:19–20, Micah 1:3–4, Zechariah 14:4–5, Matthew 27:50–54, Acts 16:25–26, Revelation 6:12–17.

Life Application and Closing Summary

What does the message of this prophet have to do with my life today?
Micah was a prophet who was not only given messages to speak, but God also asked him to humble himself while he spoke the message. Unlike Jonah, whose physical traits of skin and hair had been radically and forever changed without his choosing, Micah had to *daily choose* to humble himself and walk about barefoot and naked while he proclaimed God's messages of warning.

It was a hard message to speak because people don't like to have their sins pointed out. Throughout the book, Micah uses the words *sin* and *iniquity*. These words are almost always linked in Scripture. Compare: Psalm 38:18; Isaiah 53:5–6, 59:12; Hosea 4:7–8, 8:13, 9:9.

In Micah 2:6, people told Micah to be quiet, but he said that if God's prophets (*you*) don't speak out then "reproaches"—God's judgment cannot be turned back. If not you, then who will tell others about the goodness of God now before they see His wrath and judgment? *Today* is the day of salvation!

Take a good look at your life right now and rate yourself in the following areas:

1—Not true   5—True some of the time   10—True most of the time

___I read and study God's Word every day so I gain strength and courage to do/say what is right.

___I humble myself and obey God's direction in my daily life choices.

___I tell others about the goodness of God and talk freely about spiritual things.

___I am kind to others and work to bring justice to the wrongs that I see.

___I treat my family well and give honor to my parents/elders.

___I am quick to confess my sins and turn away from those iniquities that have caused my family trouble.

We all have room for improvement and none of us are perfect. God looks at the heart attitude, and as long as you are willing and wanting to change, the Spirit will continue to talk to you about those areas in your life where you are weakest.

Challenge for the Week

Pray and ask the Spirit to point out one area of weakness that He wants to change in you. Look up verses that talk about that specific area and memorize one or more of them. Read them every day to encourage and commit yourself to allow the Spirit of God to change your life in the weeks and months to come.

The Book of Hosea

It is very important to begin each study session with a prayer to invite the Holy Spirit of God to open your mind and heart to hear what He wants to say today.

Holy Spirit,

Thank You for inspiring the men who wrote down the words of God in these books. I agree that the Bible contains everything I need to know to live my life with peace and joy, both with God and other people. My mind and heart are open for Your direction and I will be still and quiet as I watch to see what You want to tell me today. May Your truth be a seed that is planted deep in my soul, that I may change and grow more to be like Jesus. I will delight in Your Word and meditate on it day and night as You bring it to my mind. I ask this in the name of Jesus, for His glory and my good. Amen.

In this book, God uses Hosea's marriage to Gomer as a living parable (12:10) to the people of Israel and Judah. Real life lived out in ugliness and pain; an example of God's great love and care for His people but their disloyalty and rebellion in choosing to run after other things/people to meet their needs. After two hundred years of idol worship, they had totally forgotten about God, so their actions brought punishment upon themselves (2:13, 8:13). They were in the "wilderness of slavery" (Egypt=slavery) so that they would finally remove the old habits of idol worship (2:17, 3:4) and be drawn back into a loving relationship with God (2:18–23). God then promises to restore everything back to His people that they had lost (3:5). Hosea's name means "salvation," which is apt since God uses him as a foreshadow of Jesus when he bought Gomer back off the slave block (3:2) just as Jesus bought us back from being slaves to Satan.

We are not told where Hosea is from or lived, only that he was the son of Beeri and a prophet to the northern kingdom of Israel during the reigns of the kings listed below.

Jereboam II	2 Kings 14:23–27	Israel	bad king	793–753	Hosea/Amos
Uzziah					Hosea/
(Azariah)	2 Kings 14:21	Judah	good king	792–740	Isaiah/Amos
Jotham					Hosea/
(Jothan)	2 Kings 15:32	Judah	good king	750–732	Isaiah/Micah
					Hosea/
Ahaz	2 Kings 16:1	Judah	bad king	746–711	Isaiah/Micah
					Hosea/
Hezekiah	2 Kings 18:1	Judah	good king	711–697	Isaiah/Micah

Note: In this book, the northern kingdom of Israel is also called Ephraim (younger son of Joseph) as that is the inherited tribal land in which Samaria was located (Genesis 48:11–22; Joshua 24:32; John 4:5).

In chapters 1 and 2, God tells Hosea to take a harlot (prostitute) for a wife and take care of other men's children as his own. Hosea obeys God's direction and chooses a woman named Gomer to be his wife. She gives birth to three children, all by other men (1:2, 2:4–5), and God names the children Himself. Fill in the information below:

Child	**Name**	**Meaning**
1. Boy		
Why this name?		
Hosea 1:4		
2 Kings 9:16–37		

Child	Name	Meaning
2. Girl		
Why this name?		
Hosea 1:6		

Child	Name	Meaning
3. Boy		
Why this name?		
Hosea 1:9		

Note that God takes each child's name and changes the negative into a positive.
Hosea 2:23 NASB: "And **I will sow** her [Jezreel] for Myself in the land. **I will also have compassion** [Ruhamah] on her who had not obtained compassion. And **I will say** to those who were not My people, 'You are My people!' And they will say, 'Thou art my God!'" (name denotations and emphasis mine).

Bonus study of other people that God named: Genesis 16:11, 17:5, 15, 19, 32:28; Luke 1:13, 31; Matthew 16:18.

In chapter 3, we are told that Gomer had left Hosea and the children and gone after other men to give her the things she thought she needed. Gomer ends up on the slave block where Hosea finds her and buys her back again. He tells her that from now on she will stay home and be true to him only and he will be true to her. He gives conditions/requirements of what he expects from her. Again, this is a wonderful picture of God's love and care for His bride, the church. He has purchased us for Himself by the blood of Jesus from the slave block of sin, but He has requirements of us in the relationship. Boundaries are set for *our* good, and He promises that even when we are not true and faithful to Him, He is *always* faithful to us! (1 Corinthians 1:9; Timothy 2:13; Revelation 19:11).

Write down what these verses say about God's love for Israel and Jesus's love for the church:

Hosea 2:19–20

Isaiah 54:5–8

Matthew 9:15

Ephesians 5:25–27

1 Corinthians 6:20

Romans 9:24–26

Revelation 19:7–9

Throughout the book of Hosea, God lists the wrongs that the people have committed, and in the next verse or chapter, He tells of His great love for them and that He will bless them and bring them back to Himself. Like a good parent (He calls Ephraim His son), God tells them what they have done wrong and the consequences that follow their wrong choices. (Sound familiar to the blesses and curses in Deuteronomy 28?)

Chapter 4–13. List Ephraim's sins from the following verses:

4:1

4:2

4:12

5:2

5:5

5:10

6:7

7:1

7:8

7:11

8:3

11:12

What happens when there is no knowledge of God (Hosea 4:1, 6, 14)?

List some ways you see this in our world today:

What does the Bible say is the answer (Proverbs 1:7, 22–23, 33, 2 [whole chapter])?

Life lesson: Sin becomes an iniquity (addiction) that we can't stop even when we want to because it has opened a door for an evil spirit's (demon) influence in that area of our lives. It has gone from a choice to commit sin into a bondage from which we cannot free ourselves (2 Timothy 2:26; Romans 6:17–23; Hebrews 2:14–15).

What do these passages say about Ephraim's sins and the result? Hosea 5:4, 6, 13–15; Isaiah 28:1, 7–8, 13; Psalms 7:1–11; 2 Chronicles 7:19–20.

"He will revive us after two days; He will raise us up on the third day That we may live before Him." (Like Jesus!) (Hosea 6:2a NASB).

God says He is willing to heal Israel if they would turn back to Him. Write below what these scriptures say: Hosea 6:1–3, 6, 7:1–2; 2 Chronicles 7:14; Job 5:17–18; Proverbs 3:11–12; Jeremiah 30:12–17, 31:17–19; Hebrews 12:9–13; James 5:16; Revelation 3:19.

"And they do not consider in their hearts That I remember all their wickedness. Now their deeds are all around them; They are before My face." (Hosea 7:2 NASB) Do you realize that God sees everything you do and that nothing is hidden from Him? Do you need to repent of something? Is the Holy Spirit bringing something to your mind right now? If so, stop and confess it to the Lord. He already knows and He is willing to cleanse and heal you right now (Read Hebrews 10:19–22; 1 John 1:5–10).

List all of the *similes* found in chapter 7: *Ephraim is like/has become…*

Example (v. 4): an oven whose fire is going out before the bread has even risen.

Verse 6

Verse 7

Verse 8

Verse 11

Verse 16

> Life lesson: When we are heavily into our sinful
> addictions, we change internally as well as externally
> and we don't even realize it (Hosea 7:9)!

*Sad comment: "They turn, but not upward..." (Hosea 7:16a
NASB)*

List the sins of Israel (sowing the wind) in Hosea 8 and 2 Kings
17:5–23.

List what God says will happen to them as a result (reaping the
whirlwind).

*Whirlwind = Anything moving forward and whirling with vio-
lence and force.*[20]

God is like a whirlwind in judgment. Compare Isaiah 66:15, Nahum 1:3, Psalm 77:15–19, Proverbs 1:27, and Jeremiah 23:19–20.

Bonus study on principle of sowing and reaping: God has said that as long as the earth remains, there will be seed, time, and harvest (Genesis 8:22). This principle was the same in Jesus's day and for the early church; therefore it is still the same for us today! Compare Hosea 8:7, 10:12; Matthew 13:1–30, 37–43; Luke 6:37–38; 1 Corinthians 9:11; 2 Corinthians 9:6–15; Galatians 6:7; Revelation 14:14–19.

Chapter 9 equates captivity in Assyria to Israel's slavery in Egypt. List the "normal" things of their lives that they will lose during captivity in the following areas:

Personal:

Spiritual:

In Hosea 9:9 and 15, God says that the people are deep in depravity and He will love them no more. After reading what the people were like in the 2 Kings passage, as well as Hosea 8 and 9, you get a better idea of how bad life was (especially for the children). It's hard to imagine that they were worse than the people whom God destroyed in the flood (Genesis 6) or even those in Sodom and Gomorrah (Genesis 19), but I'm sure that God was tempted to bring another flood or rain fire and brimstone again. It is only by His grace and mercy that He continues to discipline His children instead of destroying them (Malachi 3:6)!

You may not feel like your sin is as bad as that of Israel, but God sees *all* sin as rebellion against Himself. Is there an area in your life that the Spirit of God has been convicting you? If so, don't wait. Stop now and confess your sin; repent and be washed in the forgiving blood of Jesus (Read Psalm 51:1–12)!

Hosea 10 describes what Israel used to be like, but through the choices they made, everything they had will be taken from them or destroyed. The principle of sowing and reaping appears again in verse 12. *Rewrite the verse in your own words below.*

(Fallow ground is earth that has been idle—not planted and growing whatever comes up without purpose.)[21]

How does God describe His relationship to Israel/Ephraim?

11:1

11:3

11:4

11:8

Note: Admah and Zeboiim were neighboring cities to Sodom and Gomorrah that were also destroyed in the fallout of the rain of fire and brimstone (Genesis 14:8 and Deuteronomy 29:23).

Chapter 12 describes how Israel made contracts with other nations to support themselves (going after the east wind). List their business practices found in the verses below:

12:1

12:7

What did God say about the role of prophets?

12:10

12:13

> Baby Christians (new believers) often argue and contend with others (12:3) because they have not yet learned to trust God for what they need. Mature Christians argue, contend, and wrestle with God (12:4) (just like Abraham in Genesis 18:23–33 and Amos 7:1–9) because they understand that they are in a relationship with the One who can supply their every need and change their lives and circumstances.[22]

List the sins of Ephraim and what will happen to them because of their sin (Hosea 13).

> Steps into sin: You have what you want and become satisfied ->Your heart becomes proud -> You forget God (Hosea 13:6).

Does Hosea 13:14 sound familiar to you? Look up 1 Corinthians 15:50–58. Why is Paul quoting from Hosea? Does knowing that death has no power and therefore you don't need to fear it help you live your life any differently? Why or why not?

Hosea 14 is *beautiful!*
Return to God *and take* words *with you!*

Tell Him your sin and *give* Him the *fruit* of your *lips* (confession and repentance).
Acknowledge/agree that no one else can/will save you. (Jesus is the *only way* to God.)

Acknowledge/agree that the work of your hands, i.e., deeds, are not your god. (God meets your needs.)
Acknowledge/agree that we only find mercy in Him. (Thankfulness)
Be healed. (Believe it and claim it for yourself.)
Be loved. (Believe it and claim it for yourself.)
Blossom and grow. (Allow the Spirit of God to change your life.)
Be a sweet fragrance to the world. (Be a blessing to everyone you meet.)
It is God who produces the fruit in/for us (not our own efforts).
Whoever is wise, let him *understand* these things.
Whoever is discerning, let him *know* them.
For the ways of the *Lord* are *right.*
The righteous *will walk* in them.

Life Application and Closing Summary

What does the message of this prophet have to do with my life today?
Have you noticed the trend yet? Each prophet has been asked to do something that they didn't want to do or something that would bring personal discomfort/upset to their own lives. Are you willing to be an obedient prophet no matter the personal cost?

In this book, Hosea is asked to give up the rights/plans for his own life to do a *very* hard thing: To obey God in all things and trust that God will take care of his future. God has plans for good and not for evil, to give you a future and a hope (See Jeremiah 29:11)!

Questions to Ponder

Is there an area in your life that God has asked you to give Him? What was your response?

As the church, we are Jesus's bride. Have you been faithful to Him? Are you committing adultery with the world? Mixing with the nations? In your entertainment choices: TV, books, movies, websites, etc.?

Gomer purposefully left Hosea's protection and ended up in slavery. Have you ever purposefully wandered away from God? Where did you end up?

Hosea 2:8 and 11:3 NASB share a similar heart breaking picture of God. *"She/They didn't know it was ME…"* (Emphasis mine) The book of Hosea is all about God's huge love for His people and His desire to care for them, but they continually left Him for passing pleasures and soon they no longer recognized Him. In the New Testament, they didn't recognize Jesus as their Messiah either. How do you recognize God when He is in the midst of your life?

Challenge for the Week: Sowing and Reaping

Acts 10:38 tells us that Jesus went about doing good and sowed seeds of kindness into the lives of everyone He met. How much more should we now, with the Holy Spirit living within us, go about sowing good seeds *on purpose* with a goal of kindness and being a blessing to others (Hosea 10:12, 12:6)?

How can you reap if you aren't sowing, and what will you have for good seed if you aren't in the *Word* of God on a daily basis? List below specific actions you can take this week to purposely sow kindness into the lives of others.

The Book of Obadiah

It is very important to begin each study session with a prayer to invite the Holy Spirit of God to open your mind and heart to hear what He wants to say today.

Holy Spirit,

Thank You for inspiring the men who wrote down the words of God in these books. I agree that the Bible contains everything I need to know to live my life with peace and joy, both with God and other people. My mind and heart are open for Your direction, and I will be still and quiet as I watch to see what You want to tell me today. May Your truth be a seed that is planted deep in my soul, that I may change and grow more to be like Jesus. I will delight in Your Word and meditate on it day and night as You bring it to my mind. I ask this in the name of Jesus, for His glory and my good. Amen.

The meaning of Obadiah's name is "servant or worshipper of Yahweh."

There is varying opinion on when this book was written as there are several "Obadiahs" in the Old Testament and we are not given any familial connections for the writer. But because the destruction of Judah is mentioned in verses 11 and 12, it is generally thought to take place during the reign of Zedekiah when Jerusalem was destroyed by the Babylonians in 586 BC.[23]

It is the shortest of the Minor Prophet books with only one chapter containing twenty-one verses. It is also one of the few books that contain only one message to one nation: the nation of Edom—Israel's cousins that have descended from Esau.

What does God say about the character of Edom's people and where they live (verses 1–4)?

Edom included the rocky range of mountains east of Israel, stretching about one hundred miles in length and about twenty miles wide. It was well watered with good grasslands surrounded by high cliffs that overlooked the valley. The famous city of Petra was in Edom. They liked to raid other nations for supplies, etc., and then return to their hiding places in the cliffs where no armies could approach without being seen.[24]

What sins had Edom done to other nations that God said now would happen to them (verses 5–7)?

What reasons are given for God to destroy Edom (verses 10–14)?

What will their judgment be (verses 15–21)?

Within four years after Jerusalem was burned, Edom was raided and destroyed by the Babylonians in 582 BC.[25]

What do these other scriptures have to say about the judgment of Edom? Isaiah 34:5–15; Jeremiah 19:7–22; Ezekiel 25:12–14, 35:1–15; Joel 3:19; Malachi 1:1–4; Amos 1:11–12.

Just as we have natural laws such as gravity, etc., so too God has natural laws such as sowing and reaping. Compare verse 15 with Job 4:8, Exodus 34:7, and Galatians 6:7–10. What do you learn about sowing and reaping?

In Obadiah we see that what began in Esau's heart, the hate against his brother Jacob, was a seed that grew into a root of bitterness and hatred that carried down through multiple generations until it became a part of the nation's identity. See Hebrews 12:15 and Ephesians 4:31–32.

What do these *Old Testament* scriptures say about your treatment of others? Job 31:29–32; Psalm 35:26, 59:12–13; Proverbs 17:5, 24:17–18.

What do these *New Testament* scriptures say about your treatment of others? Matthew 5:22–24; Romans 14:13; James 4:11–12; 1 John 3:12, 4:20–21.

Life Application and Closing Summary

What does the message of this prophet have to do with my life today? Are you angry or bitter at someone who you feel has "done you wrong"? Are you passing this root of bitterness on to your children and grandchildren?

How do you treat your family members and how do you talk about them to others?

When they are in trouble, what is your attitude and/or response?

How do you treat your church family members and how do you talk about them to others?

When they are in trouble, what is your attitude and/or response?

Heart attitudes become actions, ways of treating other people, that set an example for future generations to follow without ever knowing why they think the way they do.

Challenge for the Week

Read Matthew 5:21–25 and apply it to your relationships. Do you need to contact someone to ask their forgiveness or to tell them that you forgive them? If the Spirit is putting a name in your mind, repent and agree with Him that your attitude and actions have been wrong and then obey and contact that person this week! When the Spirit brings conviction, He also gives the power to obey! Make sure to pray before you contact the person and ask for the Spirit to anoint your words and give you favor. The final step is to *let it go*. Satan will "offer" you bad thoughts again, but you must continue to let it go every time until he gives up!

The Book of Nahum

It is very important to begin each study session with a prayer to invite the Holy Spirit of God to open your mind and heart to hear what He wants to say today.

Holy Spirit,

Thank You for inspiring the men who wrote down the words of God in these books. I agree that the Bible contains everything I need to know to live my life with peace and joy, both with God and other people. My mind and heart are open for Your direction and I will be still and quiet as I watch to see what You want to tell me today. May Your truth be a seed that is planted deep in my soul, that I may change and grow more to be like Jesus. I will delight in Your Word and meditate on it day and night as You bring it to my mind. I ask this in the name of Jesus, for His glory and my good. Amen.

Author information: Nahum was from the city of Elkosh, which was located on the Tigris river about twenty miles north of Nineveh. This is the only personal information we are given. We don't know if he was a prophet by "trade" or a layman that God called to be a prophet.

Meaning of his name: consolation. His name is in the name "Capernaum," which means "village of Nahum," so it may indicate that he was the founder of this city by the Sea of Galilee.[26] Read these scriptures and note what role this village played in the life of Jesus: Matthew 4:13, 11:23; John 2:12, 6:17, 24.

Nahum begins by calling his book an "oracle of Nineveh." The entire book of prophecy is about the city of Nineveh. It takes place one hundred years after Jonah's successful "missionary trip." Thebes (No-amon) fell in 663 BC (Nahum 3:8–10), and the fall of Nineveh (Assyria's capital) was in 607 or 612 BC (date is contested). The book of Nahum was written sometime between these two events.

Definitions:

Oracle: burden

Burden: (a) something that is carried; (b) something that is difficult to bear physically and or emotionally[27]

Nineveh was a brutal nation who did awful things to their prisoners to inspire terror in their enemies. Their policy was to deport conquered peoples to other lands in order to destroy any ties to their homeland and national traditions (much like Babylon and what happened in the book of Daniel).[28]

Nahum 1:1 says that the burden was a vision—a scary dream in full Technicolor with vivid descriptions like an action movie where the bad guys (Assyrians) are destroyed and the hero (God) frees the hostages (the entire nation of Israel). Marvel comics might have called it "God the Avenger."

List below how God is described in Nahum 1:1–14:

Nahum 1:5 talks about earthquakes occurring in God's presence. This is why every time the Bible describes the "Day of the LORD," there are earthquakes (Ezekiel 38:18–20). When Jesus returns with His heavenly army, His feet will touch the Mount of Olives, the earth will quake, and the mountain will split in two (Zechariah 14:4–5).

Nahum 1:9–12 describes the king of Nineveh as a man who plans evil and a wicked counselor. What does verse 14 says God will do to him?

List below the description of the siege war against Nineveh found in Nahum 2:3–13 and 3:1–19.

Mantelet is a mobile screen or shield used to protect soldiers.[29]

Nahum 2:11 and 13 describe the Assyrians as lions tearing their prey. The Assyrian sculptures that have been found in archaeological dig sites all have lions in various forms depicted on them, so they were probably used as their national symbol.[30]

Bonus study on Sennacherib, king of Assyria: 2 Kings 18–19, 2 Chronicles 32:1–22, Isaiah 36–37.

The book of Nahum is a scary and violent message to the people of Nineveh (just like Jonah's) but full of good news for God's people as they hear what God is going to do to their enemies/captors. List the good news from the verses below:

1:2

1:3

1:7

1:9

1:10

1:11

1:13

1:15

The book ends with the reminder that Nineveh would reap back all the evil that she had sown into other nations. Compare with Job 4:8–11, Obadiah 1:15, Hosea 10:13–14, Galatians 6:7
Life Application and Closing Summary

What does the message of this prophet have to do with my life today?

Nahum 1:7. God is good! A stronghold in the day of trouble and He knows the name of each person who takes refuge in Him (Psalm 5:11–12, 9:9–10, 37:30–40).

What comfort/encouragement can you apply to your life from these verses?

God brings good news of peace and deliverance for His people (*you*) (Nahum 1:15; Isaiah 52:7; Luke 2:10–14; Romans 10:12–15).

God's good news *always* brings peace with it. Are you at peace today? What good news do you need to claim over your life right now and thank God for the peace it provides you?

Thought to Ponder

Is God your movable shield (mantelet)? Have you seen Him save and protect you in your life? Do you have a story to share with others—your testimony of the goodness of God?

Challenge for the Week

Look around you for someone who needs to hear about God's good news of peace and deliverance and share it this week!

Nahum 1:8 promises that God will make a complete end of Nineveh. I encourage you to read more information about the fall of Nineveh in *Halley's Bible Handbook* (pages 369–371).

The Book of Zephaniah

It is very important to begin each study session with a prayer to invite the Holy Spirit of God to open your mind and heart to hear what He wants to say today.

Holy Spirit,

Thank You for inspiring the men who wrote down the words of God in these books. I agree that the Bible contains everything I need to know to live my life with peace and joy, both with God and other people. My mind and heart are open for Your direction, and I will be still and quiet as I watch to see what You want to tell me today. May Your truth be a seed that is planted deep in my soul, that I may change and grow more to be like Jesus. I will delight in Your Word and meditate on it day and night as You bring it to my mind. I ask this in the name of Jesus, for His glory and my good. Amen.

Author information: Zephaniah was the great-great-grandson of King Hezekiah of Judah, so King Josiah was a blood relative. Second Kings 18 and 2 Chronicles 29 and Matthew 1:10 don't list Hezekiah's sons other than Manasseh who was twelve years old when he became king. Here is his lineage: Hezekiah-> Amariah-> Gedaliah-> Cushi-> Zephaniah.

Note: The book of Hosea ended at the reign of Hezekiah, so this book is four generations later.

Meaning of his name: Jehovah has concealed or Jehovah of darkness.

The main theme of the book is God's wrath and judgment on Judah. Compare these scriptures and note the similarities below: Zephaniah 1:1–3, 18; Genesis 6:5–7; 2 Peter 3:7, 10.

> Zephaniah's prophesies about the Day of the Lord's wrath and judgment on Judah and other nations were written only a few years before they were fulfilled the first time— captivity. Many of them will have their final fulfillment in the last days when Jesus returns to the earth.

List below all those who are to be judged (Zephaniah 1:4–6).

Baal was the "chief" Canaanite deity. The word Baal means "lord" or "owner" in Hebrew. 1 It was King Solomon who first built a temple for the worship of Milcom (Molech) as well as many other gods (1 Kings 11:1–13). His sin is why the tribes were torn apart. How could the wisest man on earth fall so far? (By taking foreign wives.) Ecclesiastes 12:13–14 shows that at the end of his life, Solomon knew that he would have to answer to God for all of his actions, both good and evil. It was a relative of Zephaniah, King Josiah, who destroyed the places of worship that Solomon had built to other gods.[31]

Bonus study on Milcom/Molech god of the Ammonites: Leviticus 20:2–5; 1 Kings 11:4–13, 33; 2 Kings 23:1–13; Jeremiah 32:35; Psalms 106:37–39.

Note: God judged both true and false priests the same because adding other types of worship (stars, etc.) and not seeking Him was the same to God as the sins of human sacrifice, etc.

How does this apply to you today? The sin of God and _____

Have you ever gone to a psychic? Had your palm read? Do you read/ follow your horoscope/sign? Do you watch TV shows or read books that are based on the occult? Read Leviticus 20:6–7 and write out what God says about a person who does these things.

If you answered "yes" to any of these questions, you have opened a door to Satan and given him a foothold in your life. You need to repent of it and not do it anymore but also cast any demonic influences out through the power and authority of Jesus's name. It is wrong to seek guidance for your life from ungodly sources and allow these things into your mind and heart. It deeply offends God and uncovers you from His protection.

I recently experienced a personal example of this. I was watching an interesting TV show about Alcatraz when they started talking about ghosts that lived there and how they had a "medium" that would speak to the ghosts, etc. The Holy Spirit alerted me and I realized right then that I needed to turn the channel because if I continued to watch, I would be in disobedience to the Holy Spirit and opening up myself to demonic influences. I changed the channel but also quickly confessed to God that I didn't want to open up myself to demons and claimed the blood of Jesus over my life and my home and demanded that they leave in Jesus's name. Demons are *real* and they only need a small door of opportunity to come in and affect your life. Don't do anything that invites them in, and the first step is what you put in front of your eyes and allow into your mind.

Compare these scriptures: Genesis 4:7; Luke 9:1; Acts 16:16–19; Ephesians 4:17–19, 27; Philippians 4:8; James 3:15–17; James 4:4, 7; 1 Peter 5:8–9.

Bonus study, demons are real: Deuteronomy 32:17; Matthew 4:24, 8:16, 33, 9:32–33, 12:24–29; Luke 8:26–33, 10:17–20; 1 Corinthians 10:20–21; 1 Timothy 4:1; James 2:19; Revelation 9:20–21.

Zephaniah says that the Day of the *Lord* is near and the *Lord* has prepared a sacrifice and consecrated His guests. Compare this to Isaiah 1:16–18, 62:1–5; Matthew 25:1–13, Ephesians 5:25–27; Hebrews 10:22–25; Revelation 19:7–9, 22:7–17.
Who is the Bridegroom?

Who is the sacrifice?

Who is the bride?

Who are the guests?

Who consecrates/cleanses the guests and the bride?

Do you see how much God loves His people and the lengths He goes to draw His people into a personal and intimate relationship with Himself (Read John 3:16)?

Who are the people that will receive the worst of God's punishment? What is their role?

Zephaniah 1:8, 3:3; Isaiah 2:6–8; Proverbs 23:1–8; Daniel 1:3–5, 8a

Zephaniah1:9, 3:4; Ezekiel 8:8–12

Zephaniah1:10–11; Matthew 21:12 (Fish gate, Second Quarter, and Mortar represent the merchant districts)

> Note: It is those in positions of power
> who are held most accountable.

How does Zephaniah 1:12–13 apply to your life today?

Definition: stagnant—not moving or flowing, without current, motionless. Foul from standing still, polluted, stale.[32]

Is your spiritual life stagnant? Are you allowing the Spirit of God to wash you with the water of the *Word* every day, doing something new and fresh within you? What God gives to you must then be allowed to flow out to others! The Dead Sea has no outlet, so the level of minerals build up until no living thing can survive. You must have an outlet to allow the blessings of God to flow from you to others that need it, which in turn makes room in your life for new blessings to flow in. If you don't, you too could become a dead sea.

The Day of God's wrath is coming. Compare these scriptures and note what it says about the day: Zephaniah 1:14–18; 1 Corinthians 3:13–15; Matthew 24:42, 46–51; Revelation 20:11–13.

God is a hiding place of protection for His people. What do you learn from these texts? Zephaniah 2:1–3; Psalms 17:7–8, 27:5, 32:7; Jeremiah 29:12–14; Colossians 3:3.

From Zephaniah 2 list the nations besides Israel that will be punished.

2:4–7

2:8–11

2:12–15

What does God say to them in Isaiah 45:18–22?

"The Day" is written over fifteen times in this short three-chapter book of prophecy. The first "Day of judgment" happened soon after this book was written. Each nation listed was overrun/destroyed by their enemies. The second "Day of judgment" is still to come.

Bette Midler had a popular song called "From a Distance" and the lyrics said that God is at a distance and the world is small and insignificant in His sight. Have you slid into this worldview of God? Do you believe that He doesn't care about what is happening in our world or in your own life? Do you live like you believe your actions matter and that a final day of judgment is coming?

Zephaniah 3:1–2 NASB says, "Woe to her who is rebellious and defiled, The tyrannical city! She [Jerusalem—Judah] heeded no voice; She accepted no instruction. She did not trust in the LORD; She did not draw near to her God" (notation mine).
Definition: Rebellious—resisting management or control, unruly.[33]

Thought to Ponder

Do you have a problem with rebellion, not wanting anyone to tell you what to do or have authority over your actions? Are you afraid to let God be the "boss" of your life?

Compare what these texts have to say about the positive side of obedience: Zephaniah 3:7, Psalm 32:8–9, Proverbs 8:10–11, Isaiah 1:18–20, Jeremiah 7:23–24, Romans 13:1–2.

> God's timetable is different than ours. He often says to wait, and while it seems to us that He is taking a long time to bring our answer, we can trust that even though He is never early, He is also never late.

What do these scriptures say about waiting for God? Zephaniah 3:8, Psalm 27:14, Isaiah 40:31, Daniel 12:7–12, 2 Peter 3:9–10.

Zephaniah 3:9 reminds us that only God can purify our lips, cause our words to be blessings instead of curses. See what these other passages say about our lips (words): Isaiah 6:5a, 7; James 3:8–10.

Shame affects many people today. It is often not even their own actions but what others such as parents, teachers, coaches, and others have done to them that caused them to think there is something wrong with them. God promises to remove our shame. Write down what you learn about shame below (Zephaniah 3:11; Psalm 25:1–3; Isaiah 50:7–8; 54:4, 61:7).

The name of the Lord (I AM, Jesus) is a refuge (safe place) for His people. It is the *name* of Jesus that has power to save, heal, and forgive. What does the Bible say about the name of God (Zephaniah 3:12; Psalm 5:11–12; John 14:13–14; Acts 3:16; Philippians 2:9–11)?

God always leaves Himself a remnant—a 10 percent tithe of His people Israel for Himself. Compare Zephaniah 3:13 to Revelation 7:4–8, 14:1–5. Is this a coincidence or the same author's writing, thousands of years apart?

The book of Zephaniah ends with a joyful note looking to the future when God will again dwell in the midst of His people as their king. He will save the lame and the outcasts and heal every disease forever. God will restore everything to Israel and be a mighty warrior against their enemies but a loving and gentle father to His children; Jesus the quiet, loving husband to His bride. Look up these scriptures to see that God is the same in the Old Testament, New Testament, and forever: Zephaniah 3:14–20, Matthew 11:4–5, Revelation 21:1–4.

Life Application and Closing Summary

What does the message of this prophet have to do with my life today?
Take time this week to reflect on the following questions with prayer and be open to hear what the Spirit of the *Lord* has to say to you.

Have I opened a door to Satan's influence through dipping into things of the occult?

In my area of leadership, am I following the Spirit's direction or making my own rules?

Have I become stagnant in my walk with God? Am I at a distance from Him in my daily life?

Is there any area in my heart, thoughts, actions where I am rebelling?

Am I waiting on God's timing or pushing my own agenda?

Does my mouth need to be purified?

Do I live like I know my deeds will be judged at the White Throne?

Brain Teaser: Josiah was eight years old and did many wonderful things during his thirty-one years as king, *but* in 2 Chronicles 34:27–28, God tells him that Judah would not go into captivity until after his death. Then in 2 Chronicles 35:20–24, he was warned not to go to war or else he would die. He went anyway and did die, thus bringing Judah's punishment much earlier than if he had lived to old age.

Question: Do you think that Josiah could have affected the outcome if he had *not* gone to war, or was his rebellion against God's message part of God's plan from the beginning? Predestination or man's choice?

The Book of Habakkuk

It is very important to begin each study session with a prayer to invite the Holy Spirit of God to open your mind and heart to hear what He wants to say today.

Holy Spirit,

Thank You for inspiring the men who wrote down the words of God in these books. I agree that the Bible contains everything I need to know to live my life with peace and joy, both with God and other people. My mind and heart are open for Your direction and I will be still and quiet as I watch to see what You want to tell me today. May Your truth be a seed that is planted deep in my soul, that I may change and grow more to be like Jesus. I will delight in Your Word and meditate on it day and night as You bring it to my mind. I ask this in the name of Jesus, for His glory and my good. Amen.

This book of prophecy was written during the period between 625 and 606 BC, early in the reign of Jehoiakim, King of Judah. The Chaldeans/Babylonians were moving westward but hadn't reached Judah yet.[34] *Note: Chaldean and Babylonian are interchanged within the scriptures in this lesson.*

639–608 BC	Josiah	good king
626 BC	Assyria greatly weakened by Scythian invasion	
625 BC	Babylon declared its independence of Assyria	

612 BC	Babylonians destroy Nineveh	
608 BC	Jehoahaz reigned three months and then taken to Egypt	
608–597 BC	Jehoiakim's wicked reign	
605 BC	Babylonians invaded Judah and took some captives	Daniel 1:1–4

Habakkuk's name means "one who clings or embraces." It is appropriate as chapter 1:1–4 tells us that Habakkuk saw this oracle (burden) as a violent movie in his head. But unlike the prophet Nahum, Habakkuk argues with God for making him watch it and questions why God allows the wicked to win in the end. Habakkuk must learn to cling to God and embrace His wisdom in dealing with Judah's sin.

List the "movie features" that Habakkuk saw in 1:2–4.

What is God's answer to Habakkuk's question of "why" (1:5)?

How does this compare with Isaiah 42:9 and Isaiah 48:3–7?

Habakkuk 1:5 is for you! You must believe that God is doing something new and amazing in your life *right now*! God says to you today: watch, observe, be astonished and full of wonder!

Bonus study of "new unimaginable things" God did: Numbers 16:28–33; Exodus 14:21–31, 16:4–18, 17:6; Joshua 10:12–14; 2 Kings 2:8–14, 20:8–11; Daniel 5:1–30, Luke 1:26–38, Acts 2:1–4.

What do you learn about God and how He does things in our world/ our lives?

Have you seen any examples of God doing a new thing in your life? That story becomes your testimony to tell others!

What is God's "new thing" coming for Judah?

From 1:6–11, list the description of the Chaldeans and their war tactics.

What does Isaiah 43:14–19 say about the Chaldeans?

Where else in the Bible does it talk about the Chaldeans? Who are some of the familiar Chaldeans (Genesis 11:28, 31, 15:7; Nehemiah 9:7; Acts 7:4; Job 1:17; 2 Kings 24:2; Daniel 2:2–13, 3:8–30)?

The Chaldeans were originally a nomadic tribe made up of very intelligent and, some would say, "sneaky" people. They would raid other nations and take them completely over when possible or they would infiltrate the ranks and take over from the inside out. Babylon is a good example of this. The Chaldeans started out as "wise men" to the kings/rulers and ended up becoming the kings/rulers of Babylon themselves. Nebuchadnezzar of the book of Daniel is a Chaldean and his grandson Belshazzar was the last Chaldean ruler before the Persians overtook the kingdom. The Chaldeans continued as servants to the new rulers as wise men and astrologers who kept astrological records for over 360 years. The wise men that came to Israel seeking the new baby king in Matthew 2 are thought to be Chaldeans.[35]

Note: Aramaic was the language of Assyria/Persia of the Old Testament. After living seventy-plus years in captivity, the Jews adopted/mingled it with their own Hebrew language and it became "Hebrew Aramaic" or "Jewish Aramaic" in the New Testament and beyond.[36]

Bonus study on adoption of Hebrew Aramaic by the Jews: 2 Kings 18:26, Isaiah 36:11, Ezra 4:7, John 5:2, 19:13, 17, 20, Acts 21:40, 22:2, 26:14.

What does Habakkuk know/understand about God's character in these verses? 1:12–2:1.

Habakkuk knows and understands God's character, but he has a hard time understanding all of His actions, so he asks God questions. It's encouraging for us to know that it's okay to ask God "why" when we don't understand, but we also have to remember that His ways are higher than our ways and His thoughts our thoughts, so we will never fully understand (Read Isaiah 55:8–9 NASB).

What does God tell Habakkuk to do with what he has seen?

Note: Habakkuk's vision showed what was to come in Israel's near future. John's visions in the book of Revelation show what is to come in *our* future. Habakkuk 2:3b NASB says "Though it tarries, wait for it; For it will certainly come, it will not delay." (See Revelation 3:11)

Question to Ponder

Do you believe that Jesus could/will come back at any moment? Are you living like you believe it? What do these texts say about His return? Luke 12:40, 1 Thessalonians 5:2–6, Revelation 1:3, 22:20.

Habakkuk 2:4b NASB "But the righteous will live by his faith" can also be found in Romans 1:17, Galatians 3:11, and Hebrews 10:38. Why do you think Paul used this verse so many times in his letters to the church?

Write down how the Chaldean/Babylonian king (Nebuchadnezzar) is described in Habakkuk 2:5–9.

What happened when Judah's king rebelled against Nebuchadnezzar (2 Kings 25:1–21; 2 Chronicles 36:15–20; Daniel 1:1–4)?

> Our personal acts of rebellion often have a wider
> ripple effect on other lives—not just our own!

What are some choices you have made that have had a negative effect on those around you?

Definition of woe: (1) deep sorrow, grief, (2) misfortune, calamity[37]

The second chapter of Habakkuk lists four woes. Write out the message of woe but then also write the message in today's language/application. See the example below:

2:9–11 *Woe to him who gets evil gain for himself and builds a fortress of stone to hide in.*
You only hurt yourself when you are selfish and cut yourself off from others.

2:12–13

2:15–17

2:18–19

List the promises found below:
Habakkuk 2:14, Numbers 14:21, Psalm 72:19, Isaiah 6:3, 11:9 *(1 message – 4 different writers = 1 author!)*. Habakkuk 2:20, Revelation 7:9–10, 8:1.

What do these verses say about God's glory? Habakkuk 3:3–4, Deuteronomy 33:2, Isaiah 6:3–4, Revelation 22:4.

What do these verses say about the power of God's creation? Habakkuk 3:5–15, Luke 21:25–26, Zephaniah 1:14–16.

The book of Habakkuk is based on a scary vision, and in 3:16, he tells us how scared he is for the future and that his "job" is to write it down as a warning for the people but then wait quietly for it to be fulfilled. Keeping this in mind, it is awesome to see his total faith in God's goodness. List below Habakkuk's "Though...Yet I will..." statements.

Though...

Yet I will...

Compare Habakkuk's statements with these scriptures: Job 1:21, 13:15a, Ecclesiastes 5:15.

Life Application and Closing Summary

What does the message of this prophet have to do with my life today?
Habakkuk ends the book with a personal testimony of sorts in 3:19 NASB. "The Lord GOD **IS** my strength, And He has made my feet like hind's feet (mountain goat–balanced and steady) And makes me walk on **MY** high places."(Notations and emphasis mine) I find it interesting that Habakkuk says my high places. I think he is saying that when he is scared and weak, he purposefully remembers all the times that God has helped him and shown His goodness in his own life. Read what David said in Psalm 18:32–36.

Think of your "high places." We call them "mountaintop" experiences now. Just by taking the time to remember the goodness of

God and the wonderful things He has done for you in the past will strengthen you in your weak/scary present situations just like it did for Habakkuk!

Challenge for the Week

Take the time to be quiet and remember the wonderful goodness of God in those "high places" of your past. Tell the Lord how thankful you are and read aloud all the "Though... and Yet I will..." statements from Habakkuk 3:17–18 and the Job passages listed above. Commit yourself to walking by faith even when the future seems scary. Habakkuk also prayed in 3:2 to be revived in the midst of the years. Are you feeling lost in in the middle of your life circumstances? Ask God to make Himself known to you in a new and fresh way today. Be quiet, wait, and watch what new thing He will do in your life today, this week, this year!

The Book of Haggai

It is very important to begin each study session with a prayer to invite the Holy Spirit of God to open your mind and heart to hear what He wants to say today.

Holy Spirit,

Thank You for inspiring the men who wrote down the words of God in these books. I agree that the Bible contains everything I need to know to live my life with peace and joy, both with God and other people. My mind and heart are open for Your direction and I will be still and quiet as I watch to see what You want to tell me today. May Your truth be a seed that is planted deep in my soul, that I may change and grow more to be like Jesus. I will delight in Your Word and meditate on it day and night as You bring it to my mind. I ask this in the name of Jesus, for His glory and my good. Amen.

Haggai's name means "to celebrate." It is very appropriate since he was a prophet to the people who chose to leave and go back to Jerusalem. They left what had been seventy years of captivity in Babylon/Chaldea and now in 536 BC were free under the rule of King Cyrus of Persia. Specifically, Haggai's message was for Zerubbabel, governor of Judah, and Joshua (Jeshua) who was the high priest. These two men led the first group back to Jerusalem with a goal to rebuild God's temple. Haggai may have been an old man when this book was written because it sounds like he was alive to see the original temple Solomon had built that was destroyed by Nebuchadnezzar (Ezra 3:12–13; Haggai 2:3). The prophet Zechariah was a young man who prophesied at the same time and place as

Haggai, so we will look at some of his prophesies that occurred amid those of Haggai during this book's study.

The book itself is only two chapters in length, but there are 6 main messages to the leaders and people who returned to Jerusalem using the words "Consider your ways" 5 times. The "prequel" to the book of Haggai is the book of Ezra, but it really starts in the book of Isaiah which was written 150 years earlier.

Take note of what God tells Isaiah 44:28, 45:1–7, 13 about King Cyrus and in the space below compare it to Ezra 1:1–4.

Historical legend told by Greek historian Herodotus says that King Cyrus's life was in danger as a child and he was rescued by shepherds and lived with them for the first 10 years of his life.[38] Cyrus lived approximately 150 years *after* the book of Isaiah was written, so Isaiah had *no idea* who he was talking about in the prophecy.

Read Ezra 1–2. What reason did King Cyrus give for his proclamation?

Who were the types of people that left captivity in Chaldea/Babylon?

Why did they return to Jerusalem?

Who helped pay for the trip and what did they donate?

How many people in total came back to Jerusalem?

This may be the first "missions trip" in history. Others were to support the trip/workers with silver, gold, goods, and cattle, as well as a freewill offering for the temple building itself.

The two main leaders of the people in this story are Zerubbabel and Jeshua/Joshua and the two main prophets are Haggai and Zechariah. What does Matthew 1:12 have to say about Zerubbabel?

Can you guess what the New Testament Hebrew version of the name Jeshua/Joshua is?

Nehemiah 12:1–16 gives the total list of the priests and Levites who returned to Jerusalem. Ezra is listed as well as Iddo. Look up Zechariah 1:1. Who is Zechariah's grandfather?

Below is a timeline of events and actions. Fill in what the texts say occurred.

536 BC–first year of Cyrus's reign: Ezra 1–2

536 BC–seventh month: Ezra 3:1–7

535 BC–second month: Ezra 3:8–4:5

529 BC: King Cyrus dies in Persia

529–522 BC: Ahasuerus/Artaxerxes/Ahashverosh begins seven-year reign (same guy, different languages) (Ezra 4:6–24, 7:1–28)

> The letters put the focus on the city being rebuilt but did *not* mention the temple. Satan will always twist the truth to divert people and disrupt God's plans.

522 BC—King Darius begins his thirty-seven-year reign in Persia.

520 BC six month day 1: Haggai 1:1–11 (Note: fifteen years have passed since they started building.)

Sixth month day 24: Haggai 1:12–15, Ezra 5:1–2

Seventh month day 21: Haggai 2:1–9, Ezra 5:3, 6:13 (This time the letter focused on the temple, not the city.)

Eighth month: Zechariah 1:1–6

Ninth month day 24: Haggai 2:10–23

Unknown timing of messages: Zechariah 3:1–7, 4:6–10

516 BC twelfth month day 3: Ezra 6:14–15

> Ezra was both priest and scribe who came in the second "exodus" via the decree from the king who followed Cyrus's reign, Artaxerxes I (note the similarity in their decrees).

Life Application and Closing Summary

What does the message of this prophet have to do with my life today?
Message 1: To Zerubbabel and Joshua, leaders: This people says the time has not come...

Has God given you something to do but you have put it on the back burner? Have you allowed the voices of others to distract and keep you from acting? Are you making excuses that this isn't the right time?

Message 2: To Zerubbabel, Joshua, and the people: Consider your ways...

Sometimes we are so "busy" in our lives doing what comes next on our "to-do list" or whatever the crisis or pleasures of the moment require that we don't stop to examine how our day is being spent. Satan *loves* a busy Christian because it means the odds of them having a daily time spent in praise, prayer, and Bible study are quite low. Mark 4:19 warns about the desires for other things entering our lives and pushing God's truth out of our daily lives. In the "The Everyday Life Bible, Amplified Bible," Mark 4:19 reads, "But the worries and cares of the world, [the distractions of this age with its worldly pleasures], and the deceitfulness [and the false security or glamour] of wealth [or fame], and the passionate desires for all the other things creep in and choke out the word, and it becomes unfruitful."

Haggai tells us the results of this type of lifestyle in 1:6 NASB: "You have sown much, but harvest little; you eat, but there is not enough to be satisfied; you drink, but there is not enough to become drunk; you put on clothing, but no one is warm enough; and he who earns, earns wages to put into a purse with holes."

Are you putting others things in your life before spending time with God? Has God been "touching" your circumstances—blowing away the little that comes your way in order that you would seek Him and give Him first place in your life?

List the "ripple effect" their sin had on the world around them found in Haggai 1:10–11.

> *Every* choice to sin brings a curse with it and it touches
> everything and everyone in your life. Jesus paid for
> *every* sin and *every* curse on the cross. Repent, confess,
> and return to holiness (Read Galatians 3:13).

Bonus study on the "ripple effect" of sin: Genesis 3:11–19, Romans 8:20–22, 1 Corinthians 15:21–22, Joshua 7:1–26, Numbers 16:1–40.

Bonus study the benefits of being in the Word on a daily basis: Psalm 1:1–3, 42:1–2, 119:33–38, 119:97–105, 119:165; Romans 12:1–2; 2 Timothy 3:15–17; James 1:25.

Message 3: To the people: I am with you…

Knowing that God is with you and will never leave you is all you really need to know! Write out Deuteronomy 31:6 and put it on your mirror to remind yourself that He is with you in your day!

In Haggai 1:14, it says that God stirred up their hearts. What is God stirring up in you? What are you stirring up in others?

Bonus study—other examples of stirring people up: 1 Chronicles 5:26; Jeremiah 51:11; Ezra 1:1, 5:1; Luke 23:5; 2 Timothy 1:6; Hebrews 10:24.

God's plan may be delayed but it cannot be thwarted. God's will *will* be done. If you are not willing to participate in His plan, He will find someone else who will!

Message 4: To Zerubbabel, Joshua, and the people: Take Courage... My Spirit is abiding in your midst—do not fear! God gives His people "pep talks." Compare these texts:

Haggai 2:4–5

Joshua 1:5–9

1 Chronicles 22:11–13

Isaiah 41:10–13

Jeremiah 1:5–10

Fear is faith that evil will happen. Courage is choosing to act even if/when you are afraid. Hope is faith that good will happen!

It is not our words that instill courage in others but God's Word that instills faith and power to obey and do what they can and then watch God do what only He can!

Bonus study—Pep talks: Deuteronomy 31:6–8, 23; Joshua 1:1–9; 1 Chronicles 17:11–27, 22:6–19; 2 Corinthians 5:6–9; 2 Thessalonians 2:13–17; Hebrews 3:12–14.

Message 5: To the priests: Consider… (Haggai 2:10–19)

God wanted them to look at their past history. Face it and then let it go. You cannot receive the good, new things of God if you won't let go of the past! To go forward, you *must* stop looking backward! Write out Philippians 3:13–14 in your own words below:

Message 6: To Zerubbabel: I AM…I WILL…I HAVE… (Haggai 2:20–23)

God had a personal message of encouragement for Zerubbabel. God had specific plans and he was chosen to be an instrument of God's power, i.e., His signet ring. A signet ring was used to seal documents to prove they were the directions of the person in power and that they were authentic. As a Christian, you too have a seal on you to prove that you are an authentic child of God. What do the following scriptures say about your seal?

Ephesians 1:13

Romans 5:15–16

Haggai 2:5

The promise to Israel is the same promise to you today. God's Spirit is abiding, dwelling, living inside of you, so there is *no* need to fear.

Challenge for the Week

Haggai's main messages are "Consider your ways" and "Take courage." Take time this week to consider your past and let it go. Consider your present and make the changes that the Spirit is putting on your heart right now. Take courage and act on the plans that God reveals to you and know that the blessings of God will ripple out from your life to bless not only you but those around you!

The Book of Zechariah

It is very important to begin each study session with a prayer to invite the Holy Spirit of God to open your mind and heart to hear what He wants to say today.

Holy Spirit,

Thank You for inspiring the men who wrote down the words of God in these books. I agree that the Bible contains everything I need to know to live my life with peace and joy, both with God and other people. My mind and heart are open for Your direction and I will be still and quiet as I watch to see what You want to tell me today. May Your truth be a seed that is planted deep in my soul, that I may change and grow more to be like Jesus. I will delight in Your Word and meditate on it day and night as You bring it to my mind. I ask this in the name of Jesus, for His glory and my good. Amen.

Zechariah was the son of Berechiah who is believed to have died in Chaldea/Babylon because Zechariah came with his grandfather Iddo, the priest in the first group of people leaving captivity in what was now called Persia to return to their homeland in Jerusalem. (We looked at several of his prophecies in the study of Haggai with messages for those people.)

It is fitting that Zechariah's name means "Yahweh (I AM) remembers" because his prophesies cover thousands of years' worth of God's activities in human lives. This is one of the longest books in the Minor Prophets, but it was written in what might be the shortest life span because we are told by Jesus that Zechariah was murdered for his prophesies. Look up Matthew 23:35 to see what Jesus said about him.

The book begins in the second year of Darius, King of Persia (whom we met in the study on Haggai) with God saying how angry He was with those He sent into captivity but that now was the time to "return to Me" and follow His ways. Read chapter 1:1–6.

The rest of the book jumps back and forth like time warps on *Star Trek*, revealing insights into things that would soon happen and many things that would happen long after the people listening were dead and dust. Because it skips around so much, we will study it by theme, not chapters.

Compare these scriptures and write what you learn below. Information for then.

Zechariah 1:18–21, Jeremiah 30:11, 16

Zechariah 2:7–9, Isaiah 48:20, Jeremiah 51:6

Zechariah 9:1–4, Ezekiel 26:2–4, 28:22–24

Zechariah 9:5–7, Jeremiah 47:4–7

Compare these scriptures and write what you learn below. Information for then and now.

Zechariah 7:2–7, Romans 14:2–6

Zechariah 7:9–10, Exodus 22:21–24, Acts 6:1–3, James 1:27, Hebrews 13:2

Zechariah 8:16–17, Proverbs 6:16–19, Ephesians 4:25

Zechariah 10:2–3, Jeremiah 14:14–16, Lamentations 2:14, 2 Timothy 4:3–4

Compare these scriptures and write what you learn below: Information for then—now—future.

Zechariah 1:7–17, 6:1–7; Revelation 6:2–8

Zechariah 1:16, 2:1–2; Ezekiel 40:3 to 43:17; Revelation 11:1, 21:15–17

Zechariah 1:20–21; Isaiah 54:16; Daniel 7:7–8, 11; Revelation 12:3, 13:1, 11

Zechariah 2:11, 8:22–23; Acts 2:5–11, 39; Revelation 7:9–10

Zechariah 3:1–2; Job 1:6–12; Revelation 12:10; Isaiah 54:17 (promise)

Zechariah 3:9, 4:2, 10; Proverbs 15:3; Revelation 1:4, 4:5, 5:6

Zechariah 5:1–4; Genesis 3:14–19; Isaiah 24:5–6; Ezekiel 2:8–10 3:2–4, 17–19; Revelation 10:8–11; Zechariah 14:11, Revelation 22:3

Zechariah 7:11–14; Mark 8:17; Romans 11:7, 25; Ezekiel 36:26–27; Hebrews 3:8–11, 15, 19, 2:1–3, 4:7

Zechariah 11:12–13, Matthew 27:3–9

Zechariah 12:10–14; Ezekiel 39:29; Luke 23:44–48; Acts 2:37; Revelation 1:7

Compare these scriptures and write what you learn below. Information for the future.

Zechariah 2:10; Mark 1:14–15; Revelation 11:15, 21:2–3

Zechariah 2:13; Habakkuk 2:20; Zephaniah 1:7; Psalm 50:1–6; Revelation 8:1

Zechariah 4:3, 11–14; Psalm 1:3, 52:8; Romans 11:17; Revelation 11:3–12

> The two witnesses will be killed, will rise from the dead after 3 ½ days, and ascend into heaven on a cloud—just like Jesus! Many scholars believe that these witnesses are Enoch and Elijah, both who never had a physical death; they were taken up into heaven by God (Genesis 5:21–24 and 2 Kings 2:1, 11).

Zechariah 5:5–11; Genesis 10:9–10, 11:1–9; Jeremiah 51:6–9; Revelation 17:4–5, 18:20, 24

Zechariah 8:3–5; Isaiah 65:17–25; Zechariah 14:8–11; Revelation 16:13–16

Zechariah 11:1–9; Matthew 25:31–32; Zechariah 12:1–9, 11:8; Revelation 16:13–16

Zechariah 13:2, 1 Kings 22:22, 1Timothy 4:1, Revelation 20:1–3

Zechariah 13:8–9, Revelation 7:4–8, 14:1–5

Ephraim and Dan's territories shared a border and were
in the region of Samaria. Both had a golden calf set
up for false worship (1 Kings 12:25–29). In the final
list of tribes in Revelation, their names are replaced by
Manasseh and Joseph instead. No remnant left?

Zechariah 14:1–3; Revelation 16:14, 19:11–19

Zechariah 14:12–18, Revelation 9:17–21

Zechariah 14:16–19, Revelation 21:24–26

*Feast of Booths and Feast of Tabernacles are the same thing. In
Hebrew it is called "Sukkot," which means temporary dwelling. Leviticus
23:34–43 describes how it is celebrated. Sukkot is still being celebrated
today by devout Jews. Families camp out in "tents" for a week and get
together for big meals to celebrate.*[39]

Compare: Information about Jesus. *(This book is second only to Isaiah
for the number of messianic prophesies in the entire Bible.)*[40]

Zechariah 3:8, Isaiah 11:1–2, Jeremiah 33:15, Revelation 22:16

Zechariah 6:11–15, Jeremiah 23:5, Hebrews 4:14–16

Zechariah 9:9–10, Matthew 21:1–9

Zechariah 10:3b–4, Ephesians 2:20–21, 1 Peter 2:5–8, Isaiah 28:16

Zechariah 11:15–17, John 10:11–15, Revelation 7:17

Zechariah 13:1; John 4:14, 7:37–38; Revelation 21:6

Zechariah 13:6–7, Luke 22:47–48, Matthew 26:31

Note: New American Standard Bible notes that the Hebrew word that is translated "arms" (Zechariah passage) means hands and that "in the house of my friends" means by those who love me. This is a vivid picture of the betrayal and the crucifixion of Jesus.

Zechariah 14:3–7, Micah 1:3–4, Acts 1:9–12, Revelation 1:7

From the book of Genesis to the book of Revelation, God tells us what He is going to do before it happens! Why is knowing information about future events important to us? Look up: Luke 12:35, Matthew 25:1–13, and Revelation 3:20 and write out your answer below.

Bonus study on the treatment of orphans, widows, and strangers (aliens): Zechariah 7:9–10, Exodus 22:21–24, Psalm 146:7–9, Malachi 3:5, Matthew 25:35–40, Hebrews 13:2, James 1:27.

Life Application and Closing Summary

What does the message of this prophet have to do with my life today?
There is *so* much going on in the book of Zechariah, and if you read it straight through, it is hard to make sense of it all. I hope that you found it easier to study the book by themes instead. Here are some things that I found interesting to think about for my life today. See what you think for yourself.

Zechariah 1 and 6 and Revelation 6 as well as Hebrews 13:2 speak of angels visiting the earth.

What do you think about the four horsemen? Are they still patrolling the earth? Yes, according to Revelation they are still being sent out to walk around and report back to God.

Do you think that you have ever entertained angels while they were on a mission to the earth? This idea totally changes how you think about treating people who are strangers to you. Be nice!

"Apple of His eye" (Zechariah 2:8c NASB). You are the center of His focus, and just as your eyelashes have a built-in system to protect

your eyeball, so God has a built in system (Holy Spirit) to protect His children from anyone that wants to harm you (Satan and the people he works through).

Intentional acts of rejection dull your ability to hear God (Zechariah 7:11–14). Has this ever happened to you in your life? Have you "cleaned your ears" lately by washing with the water of the *Word* (Ephesians 5:25b–26)?

Believe (Zechariah 8:6, Habakkuk 1:5, Jeremiah 32:27, Matthew 19:26, John 6:29, Hebrews11:6)! Just because you can't visualize something doesn't mean God can't/won't do it! *Watch, be amazed, wonder.* God is doing something in your days you won't believe! *All* things are possible with God and you *must* believe that God is able to do *anything* for those that seek Him. John tells us that *the "work of God" is to believe*. My question to you is: How is that working in your life?

Do you think this could be a description of *nuclear fallout* (Zechariah 14:12)? Do you think they might have gotten the idea for the first *Indiana Jones* movie reaction to the Ark of the Covenant from this scripture? By the way, I know exactly where the ark is right now. Look up Revelation 11:15–19.

The Book of Malachi

It is very important to begin each study session with a prayer to invite the Holy Spirit of God to open your mind and heart to hear what He wants to say today.

Holy Spirit,

Thank You for inspiring the men who wrote down the words of God in these books. I agree that the Bible contains everything I need to know to live my life with peace and joy, both with God and other people. My mind and heart are open for Your direction and I will be still and quiet as I watch to see what You want to tell me today. May Your truth be a seed that is planted deep in my soul, that I may change and grow more to be like Jesus. I will delight in Your Word and meditate on it day and night as You bring it to my mind. I ask this in the name of Jesus, for His glory and my good. Amen.

The book of Malachi is the last formal written *word* of the *Lord* for four hundred years.[41] God leaves His people with instructions to help them live wisely, safely, happily, and to be prepared for the coming Messiah—Jesus. The name Malachi means messenger, and since there is no family or locational information given about the writer (much like the New Testament book of Hebrews), there has been some discussion that it may have been Nehemiah who wrote it.[42] Other commentaries state that it is more likely that the man's name was Malachi and he was never mentioned in any other part of the Old Testament[43] (like many others who only show up once in a story, etc.).

The book was written around 450 BC to about one hundred years after the books of Ezra, Nehemiah, Haggai, and Zechariah. We can know this because in chapter 1 verses 7 and 10, the temple had already been rebuilt and sacrifices reinstated. Also, in verse 8, it says that they are under a Persian governor (not under Nehemiah's stint).[44] Sad to say in verse 6 the sins are the same as noted by Nehemiah in his second term (priests/tithes) (Nehemiah 13:4–13). In other words, people don't change easily or quickly.

This book is *not* an easy book to study because God's truths are "black and white"—they don't change. No one likes to think that they are wrong, but I pray that the Spirit of God will convict or confirm you in any area of your life that may not measure up to God's truth. Each of us will be held accountable to God alone by how we have applied the truths that are written in this book of the Minor Prophets.

The truths in Malachi reveal God's expectations of His people. These expectations have not changed just because it is two thousand-plus years later. God's truth still stands and we are not to compare them with our own experiences or feelings. God's character and His moral laws are the same yesterday, today, and forever and our society today *cannot* alter their truth.

Therefore, as you study, do not depend upon how you feel! Keep your eyes and ears open, look and listen to what truths the Spirit wants to show you, and apply them in your life today.

Truth 1: God chooses whom He will love. Look up and note what you learn from these scriptures: Malachi 1:1–5; Genesis 4:3–5, 17:18–21; Psalm 78:67–72; 1 Chronicles 28:4; 1 Peter 2:9–10; Ephesians 1:4–14.

Truth 2: God demands respect and honor from His children. Look up and note what you learn from these scriptures: Malachi 1:6–14, Psalm 51:16–17, Romans 12:1, Galatians 6:7–9, Hebrews 13:15–16.

> Notice that what bothered God the most was that His *name* was being despised by Israel and therefore by the surrounding nations as well (five times in verses 6, 11, 14). It is the *name* that has power—the *name* represents all that He is!

Bonus study on the Name of God: Exodus 3:14–15, 20:7; Leviticus 19:12; 1 Samuel 17:45; Psalm 54:1, 6; Psalm 113; John 2:23, 14:14; Mark 16:17–18; Acts 3:6, 19:13–17, 22:16; Romans 2:24; Philippians 2:9–11; 1 John 2:12 (these are just a few texts. All throughout Scripture it is the name of God that is worshipped, prayed to, sung about, exalted, etc. We need to have much more awe and fear when we use the name of God in our speech!

Truth 3: We are priests, held to a higher standard as teachers/leaders of others. Look up and note what you learn from these scriptures: Malachi 2:1–12; 1 Peter 2:5, 9; 1 Corinthians 11:27–32; 2 Timothy 2:14–16; Revelation 3:2–6.

In today's world we seem to only see negative issues with priests, but throughout the Bible, the role of priest was very important. They were in charge of all worship to God and the teaching about God. They were the "go-between" of the people and God Himself. Jesus became our high priest and now every Christian holds the office of priest as we worship and teach others about Him. (Read 1 Peter 2:9)

> The principle of *if/then* is used all over the Bible. *If* states that we have a part/role to play, an action to take, etc. *Then* shows that God also has a part/role to play, an action that He will take. Each of these *if/then* statements are rock-solid promises from God that we can claim for ourselves today. Jesus fulfilled every one of God's requirements on our behalf so we can stand back and watch what God will do for us!

Bonus study on if/then: Compare our part and God's part in these scriptures: Exodus 15:26; Joshua 1:7–8, 24:20; 1 Samuel 12:14–15; 1 Chronicles 28:9; 2 Chronicles 7:13–14; Job 22:23–30; Psalm 81:10–16; Matthew 6:14–15, 21:21–22; John 6:51; 2 Timothy 2:11–13; Hebrews 10:26–27; James 1:5; 1 John 1:9, 5:14–15.

Truth 4: God's people are held to a higher standard in marriage. Look up and note what you learn from these scriptures: Malachi 2:13–17; Genesis 2:21–24; Mark 10:2–12; 1 Corinthians 7:10–17; 1 Peter 3:7–13.

God created the marriage covenant. In the world today, the divorce rate is about 50 percent. The rate for Christians is from 26–38 percent.[45] In Mark 10:2–12, Jesus uses very strong language against divorce. Write out here what Jesus said:

Do you believe that anyone who divorces their spouse (except for adultery and/or an unbelieving spouse wants to leave) (1 Corinthians 7:10–17) and remarries commits adultery? If not, you need to read the scripture above again. It is important to remember, though, that we all sin and none of us can fully know another person's heart; the final judgment for all of our lives will be God's alone.

Do you believe that how you treat/talk to your spouse affects your relationship with God? Read Malachi 2:13–14 and 1 Peter 3:7–13 again. Do you need to repent both to God and your spouse?

Truth 5: Jesus is coming again as a judge and books are being written. Look up and note what you learn from these scriptures: Malachi 3:1–5, 4:1–6; Isaiah 66:15–16; Matthew 11:7–14, Romans 14:10–12; 1 Corinthians 3:13–15, 4:5; 1 Thessalonians 5:1–11; Malachi 3:16–18; Revelation 16:15, 20:11–15.

Note: Books, plural. There are several books we are told about in Revelation 20:11–15 and also mentioned in Daniel 7:9–10, 12:1–2 as well as in Exodus 32:32–33. The Lamb's Book of Life, the Book of Remembrance, and the myriads of biographies that contain all the actions of every human being since time began. Lots of books in heaven (Psalm 56:8, 139:16)!

God knows your name and pays attention to what you say about Him. Is your name written in His Book of Remembrance as well as the Lamb's Book of Life (Malachi 3:16)?

John the Baptist was God's chosen messenger from the beginning of creation in his mother's womb (Luke 1:5–25, 57–80) to the day of his death in prison. His job was to prepare the people to hear Jesus's message (Luke 3:1–20) by preaching repentance and a need for forgiveness of sins. Jesus came to *show* the love and grace of God for *all* the people He created (not just the Jews) and *tell* everyone that He

THE BOOK OF MALACHI

was the *only* way to God. When Jesus comes again to earth, He will *show* the holiness and righteousness of God as Judge of *all* people.

Bonus study about God's fire: Malachi 3:6, Exodus 3:1–5, Leviticus 10:2, Numbers 1:1, Deuteronomy 4:24, 2 Kings 1:10–12, 2 Chronicles 7:1, Lamentations 3:22, Ezekiel 1:26–28, Daniel 7:9–10, Luke 3:16–17, 2 Thessalonians 1:7–10, Hebrews 12:25–29, Revelation 1:13–15, 19:11–16.

Truth 6: Who God is never changes, what He does is always changing. Look up and note what you learn from these scriptures: Malachi 3:6, Hebrews 13:8, James 1:17, Revelation 1:8.

There are many scriptures where it says that God changes His mind (relents) but He does not *change His character. He told Moses, "I AM WHO I AM." (Exodus 3:14b NASB)*

Bonus study—When God "changed His mind": Genesis 18:17–33; Exodus 32:7–14; Jeremiah 18:7–10, 26:13, 19; Joel 2:13–14, Amos 7:1–6, Jonah 3:9–10, 4:2, 11.

Truth 7: God asks that His people give a tithe (10 percent) as acceptable worship. Look up and note what you learn from these scriptures: Deuteronomy 26:10–19; Malachi 3:7–15, 4:4; Haggai 1:4–11; Psalm 24:1; Matthew 5:17; Acts 4:32–37; Romans 15:26–27; Ephesians 4:28; Philippians 4:15–19.

Some people say that tithing was "under the law," but tithing actually began in Genesis 4:3–5 (Abel) and Genesis 14:18–20 (Abraham), thousands of years before the law was given to Moses on Mount Sinai. You obey God's laws all the time. You don't kill people because the law is still in effect under the law of grace! Hebrews 5:5–6 and Hebrews 7 tell us that Jesus is in the order (line) of Melchizedek who received Abraham's tithe. How much more should we show our gratitude for His provision today (Hebrews 12:28)? Matthew 6:20–21 tells us to store our treasure in heaven so that our hearts will be focused there and not on ourselves here. It does not take faith to give the last of your sheep; it takes faith to give the first one, never knowing if there will be more in the future![46]

> Robert Morris says *not* tithing = robbing/stealing = *no trust* that God is your provider. You believe that *you* can do more with 100 percent in your bank account than *God can do* with the 90 percent left in your account after the tithe is brought (to your local church—temple). Notice you *never* "give" a tithe. You can only *bring* a tithe because it already belongs to God. You can "give" an offering that is over and above your tithe, not instead of your tithe![47]

Life Application and Closing Summary

What does the message of this prophet have to do with my life today?
According to Malachi 3:8–18, how do you return to God?
Step 1: *Bring* your tithes and offerings into the local church (temple) where you worship God.
Step 2: *Serve* God with gladness in your local church and wherever God leads you.
Step 3: *Obey* the laws of God: live holy and righteous, different from the world around you.

God promises to bless you until you have no more need. Others will see God's blessing on your life and you *will be* a "delightful land." (Malachi 3:12b NASB) Malachi 4:2–3 promises healing, energy, and power for those that love and fear God. Make sure that is *you*! If you haven't been giving God the first 10 percent of your income, make a commitment to Him today. God and the church do not *need* your money; God wants your heart and He knows that where you put your money determines where your heart/attention will be. Consider the example of buying a stock. You didn't ever think about that stock before you bought it, but now you continually check on it to see what it is doing—going up or down, etc. Your attention will be on godly things if you are investing in God's kingdom here on earth! Start tithing and get involved with your local church to join God in what He is doing there!

Thoughts to Ponder

You are a priest. What are you teaching others that are watching your life? Are you a cause of offense and by your actions/words keeping others from pursuing Jesus?

Are you a willing servant, making your life a daily sacrifice in thanks to God? Do you give God your best or your leftover, damaged goods?

If life is a classroom, what "grade" would your spouse give you? Are your prayers hitting the ceiling or reaching the throne room of God?

Are you ready for Jesus to come back today? Ready for your actions/motives to be judged by fire?

Overview of the Twelve Books of the Minor Prophets

Books written precaptivity are the following: Joel, Amos, Obadiah, Jonah, Micah, Nahum, Hosea, Zephaniah.

Books written postcaptivity are the following: Haggai, Zechariah, Malachi.

"The Day / The Day of the Lord" is mentioned in seven of the books: Joel, Amos, Micah, Zephaniah, Haggai, Zechariah, Malachi.

Why is it important for you to know about "The Day of the Lord"?
Jesus *is* coming back soon, and you need to know what the Word says about it so that you cannot be fooled or confused by false teaching.

Five books are written with personal/specific messages: Jonah, Nahum, Obadiah, Hosea, Habakkuk.

The main themes of the twelve minor prophet books are the following:
Joel: Locusts and lions—judgments like the book of Revelation. Spiritual rain—prophecy.
Amos: "Woes" to the GATED JIM nations. He was a layman that was called to be a prophet.
Obadiah: Importance of how you treat your family members as well as those in the church family.
Jonah: Personal journal, lessons in life. He had a personal cost of humility.
Nahum: God is the "Avenging Hero" against Nineveh in a "movie vision."
Micah: Over sixty years of prophecy about judgment. He had a personal cost of humility.
Hosea: Living parable of "marital rebellion." He had a personal cost of love, family, and humility.
Zephaniah: Judgment is coming. Now and in "that day," this is mentioned fifteen times.

THE BOOK OF MALACHI

Habakkuk: A bad "movie" starring the Chaldeans. Conversations with God.

Haggai: Consider your ways! Take courage!

Zechariah: Prophecy like the book of Revelation. The personal cost was murder.

Malachi: God's truths for living a holy life until you next hear from God.

Closing Comments

Now that you have completed your study of the Minor Prophets, I encourage you to go back where we started in Deuteronomy 28 and look over the lists you made of the blessings and curses. Do you see how Israel and Judah brought all of those curses upon themselves and the generations that followed? So, too, blessings can and will come to all of those who love and obey God's *Word* and follow His direction for their lives.

It's important to think of God's law as "boundaries" for safe living, not a "do or don't" list.[48] We are Jesus's sheep and He leads us in and out of the sheepfold into the pastures of our daily lives. By following His voice and *only* His voice, we will dwell in safety and have the abundant life of joy that Jesus promises to give us (Psalm 23; John 10:1–11). Gentile believers have become "spiritual Jews." We have been grafted into the Jewish covenant (Romans 11), and therefore we will also receive every one of the blessings listed *if* we accept and follow His Son Jesus. Thanks be to God for His perfect gift! (Read John 4:10; Acts 2:38; Romans 6:23; 2 Corinthians 9:15; James 1:17)!

I pray that you will continue to study God's Word. As you read the Bible, remember to put yourself into the story/event and ask the Spirit of God what He wants you to see or learn from the passage. Claim any promises, obey any directions, and be encouraged by the examples of these men and women who did great and mighty things in the power of the Lord. That same power dwells inside of you if you have believed in Jesus as your Lord and Savior, and you too can do great and mighty things for God (Romans 8:11). The Word of God is still alive and active and God will use *all* of His *Word* to transform your life—if you let it.

Blessings,
Diane

If you have not yet asked Jesus to come into your life and save you from your sins and bring you into a good future with Him, here is what you need to know!

The Bible says that we are all sinful people because the very first man, Adam, sinned. Everyone born after him inherits the genetic condition to sin, and we all do and say bad things. Jesus is God's Son. He never sinned, and because He was perfect when He died on the cross, He took all of our sins onto Himself as punishment and God accepted Him in our place. The Bible also says that if we agree that we have sinned and believe that Jesus died in our place, we can ask Jesus to come and live within us. He promises that He will and that when we die, we will go to heaven to live with Him.

Jesus said, "I am the way, and the truth, and the life; no one comes to the Father, but through Me" (John 14:6 NASB).

> "For God so loved the world, that He gave His only begotten Son, that whoever believes in Him should not perish, but have eternal life. For God did not send the Son into the world to judge the world; but that the world should be saved through Him." (John 3:16–17 NASB)

> "But God demonstrates His own love toward us, in that while we were yet sinners, Christ died for us. Much more then, having now been justified by His blood, we shall be saved from the wrath of God through Him." (Romans 5:8–9 NASB)

> "That if you confess with your mouth Jesus as Lord, and believe in your heart that God raised Him from the dead, you shall be saved; for with the heart man believes, resulting in righteousness, and with the mouth he confesses, resulting in salvation." (Romans 10:9–10 NASB)

To accept Jesus into your life, pray this prayer (or one like it) *out loud*: "Dear Jesus, I believe that You are the Son of God. I believe that You died on the cross for my sins and that because You rose from the dead, when I die, I can also rise from the dead to be with You in heaven. Please come into my heart and take away all my sins: past, present, and future and give me Your Holy Spirit to help me turn away from the things that are wrong and begin to live my life to please You. Thank You that the Holy Spirit is now living in me and confirms to me that when I die, I will go to be with You in heaven. Amen."

Notes

General Information

Meaning of names and other general background information on the Minor Prophets gleaned from: Concise Old Testament Survey by J. Hampton Keathley III (hamptonk3@bible.org Biblical Studies Press, www.bible.org 1998, 7. Minor Prophets).

---

[1] *Welcome to an In-Depth Study of the Minor Prophets*
      Pastor Robert Morris Ministries daily TV program as seen on TBN 8/19/20, "Living in His Presence" sermon series.

The Book of Joel

[2] New College Edition, *The American Heritage Dictionary of the English Language* (Houghton Mifflin Company Publishing, 1976), 34.
[3] Encyclopedia Britannica, William Benton, Publisher 1969, Vol. 14, 198–199.
[4] Brady Boyd, *Speak Life, Restoring Healthy communication in how you think, talk, and pray* (David C. Cook Publishing, 2016), 22, 250.

The Book of Amos

[5] Henry H. Halley, *Halley's Bible Handbook, New Revised Edition* (Zondervan Publishing, 1965), 359.
[6] Ibid, 358.
[7] Ibid, 359.
[8] Ibid.
[9] Charles Caldwell Ryrie, *Ryrie Study Bible, New American Standard* (Moody Bible Institute of Chicago, 1978), 1363.
[10] *New American Standard Bible*, Reference Edition (Moody Press Chicago, 1975), 874.
[11] Merrill C. Tenney, *Handy Dictionary of the Bible* (Zondervan Publishing, 1971), 162.
[12] Henry H. Halley, *Halley's Bible Handbook, New Revised Edition* (Zondervan Publishing, 1965), 358.
[13] Ibid, 386.

NOTES

The Book of Jonah

¹⁴ Henry H. Halley, *Halley's Bible Handbook, New Revised Edition* (Zondervan Publishing, 1965), 363.
¹⁵ www.gotquestions.org/Jonah-whale.html, pg. 32.
¹⁶ Henry H. Halley, *Halley's Bible Handbook, New Revised Edition* (Zondervan Publishing, 1965), 365.
¹⁷ www.newhope-cf.org/21DayFast, New Hope Community Fellowship, 21 day fast, *The Principle of Fasting* definition.
¹⁸ Charles Caldwell Ryrie, *Ryrie Study Bible, New American Standard* (Moody Bible Institute of Chicago, 1978), 1380.
¹⁹ Henry H. Halley, *Halley's Bible Handbook, New Revised Edition* (Zondervan Publishing, 1965), 362, Figure 7.

The Book of Hosea

²⁰ New College Edition, *The American Heritage Dictionary of the English Language* (Houghton Mifflin Company Publishing, 1976), 1460.
²¹ Ibid, 473.
²² Joyce Meyer preaching this concept on daily broadcast of Enjoying Everyday Life.

The Book of Obadiah

²³ Henry H. Halley, *Halley's Bible Handbook, New Revised Edition* (Zondervan Publishing, 1965), 361.
²⁴ Ibid.
²⁵ Ibid, 362.

The Book of Nahum

²⁶ Henry H. Halley, *Halley's Bible Handbook, New Revised Edition* (Zondervan Publishing, 1965), 368.
²⁷ New College Edition, *The American Heritage Dictionary of the English Language* (Houghton Mifflin Company Publishing, 1976), 177.
²⁸ Henry H. Halley, *Halley's Bible Handbook, New Revised Edition* (Zondervan Publishing, 1965), 209.
²⁹ New College Edition, *The American Heritage Dictionary of the English Language* (Houghton Mifflin Company Publishing, 1976), 795.
³⁰ Charles Caldwell Ryrie, *Ryrie Study Bible, New American Standard* (Moody Bible Institute of Chicago, 1978), 1394.

The Book of Zephaniah

³¹ New College Edition, *The American Heritage Dictionary of the English Language* (Houghton Mifflin Company Publishing, 1976), 95.

[32] Ibid, 1255.
[33] Ibid, 1087.

The Book of Habakkuk

[34] Henry H. Halley, *Halley's Bible Handbook, New Revised Edition* (Zondervan Publishing, 1965), 372.
[35] Gotquestions.org. "Who were the Chaldeans in the Bible?" Bible Answers for Almost all Your Questions by Elmer Towns.
[36] Myjewishlearning.com, Languages, Jewish Aramaic.
[37] New College Edition, *The American Heritage Dictionary of the English Language* (Houghton Mifflin Company Publishing, 1976), 1472.

The Book of Haggai

[38] Ducksters.com, history, Cyrus the Great, "Ancient Mesopotamia Biography of Cyrus the Great."

The Book of Zechariah

[39] Officeholidays.com, holidays, sukkot.
[40] Charles Caldwell Ryrie, *Ryrie Study Bible, New American Standard* (Moody Bible Institute of Chicago, 1978), 1414.

The Book of Malachi

[41] Henry H. Halley, *Halley's Bible Handbook, New Revised Edition* (Zondervan Publishing, 1965), 386.
[42] *Concise Old Testament Survey* by J. Hampton Keathley III, hamptonk3@bible.org Biblical Studies Press, www.bible.org 1998, 7. Minor Prophets, Malachi.
[43] Charles Caldwell Ryrie, *Ryrie Study Bible, New American Standard* (Moody Bible Institute of Chicago, 1978), 1430.
[44] Henry H. Halley, *Halley's Bible Handbook, New Revised Edition* (Zondervan Publishing, 1965), 384.
[45] www.wf-lawyers.com, divorce statistics and facts, divorce and religion.
[46] Comments made by Pastor Robert Morris, Gateway church, during his daily broadcast of Robert Morris Ministries on TBN.
[47] Ibid.

Closing Comments

[48] Comments made by Pastor Robert Morris, Gateway church, as seen on daily broadcast of Robert Morris Ministries on TBN.

About the Author

Diane Rafferty made Jesus her Savior at the age of seven, but He became her Lord at the age of seventeen when she heard God speak to her directly from His Word.

Diane feels that her life purpose is to help people mature and grow in their love and knowledge of God's love letter—the Bible. To encourage believers in Jesus to actively seek to hear God's voice and see His power released into their daily lives as they spend time in God's Word.

Diane has been married for over thirty-nine years and lives in Washington state. She has two adult children and seven grandchildren.

CPSIA information can be obtained
at www.ICGtesting.com
Printed in the USA
LVHW091130181021
700751LV00004B/82